PIANO | VOCAL | GUITAR

SONGS FROM THE HEART

SONGS

From the

HEART

ISBN 978-1-4803-5264-3

HAL•LEONARD® CORPORATION

7777 W. Bluemound Rd. P.O. Box 13819 Milwaukee, WI 53213

Visit Hal Leonard Online at
www.halleonard.com

CONTENTS

ANNIE'S SONG

Words and Music by
JOHN DENVER

You fill up my sens - es _____

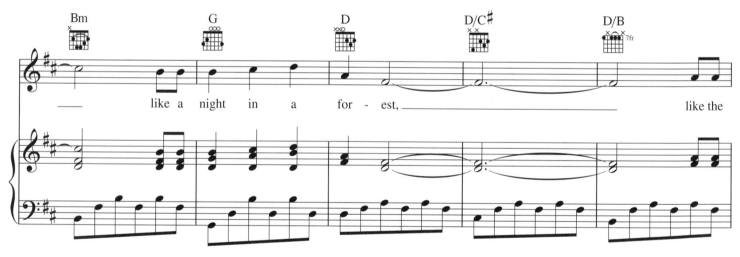

_____ like a night in a for - est, _____ like the

moun - tains in spring - time, _____ like a walk in the

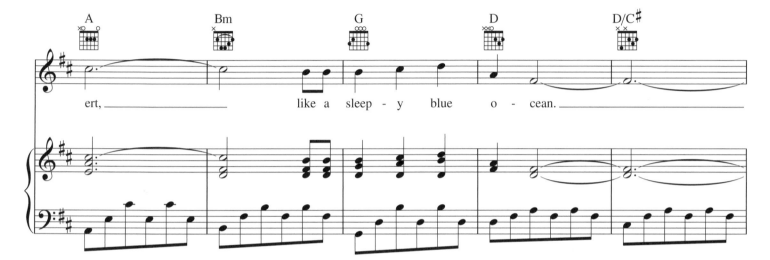

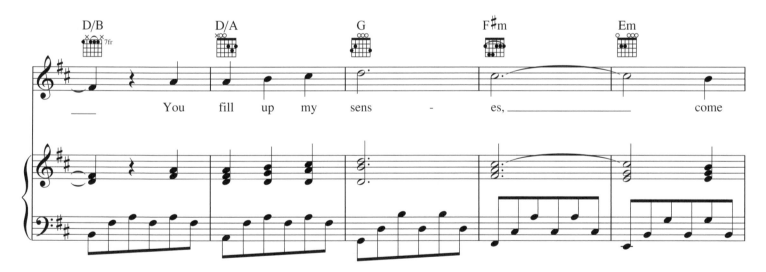

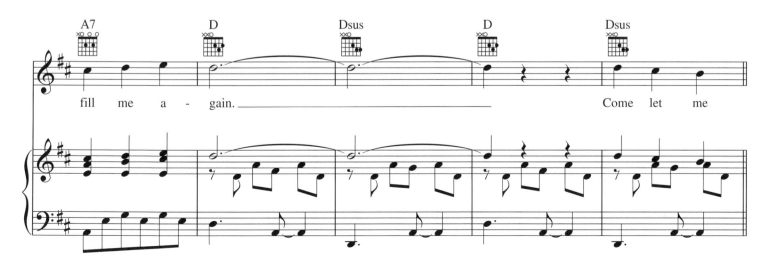

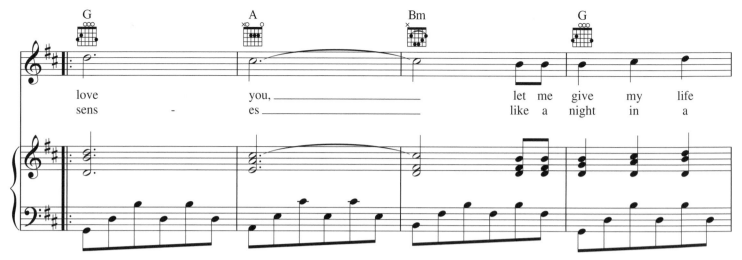

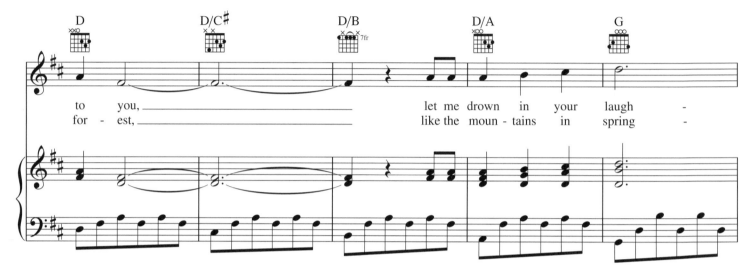

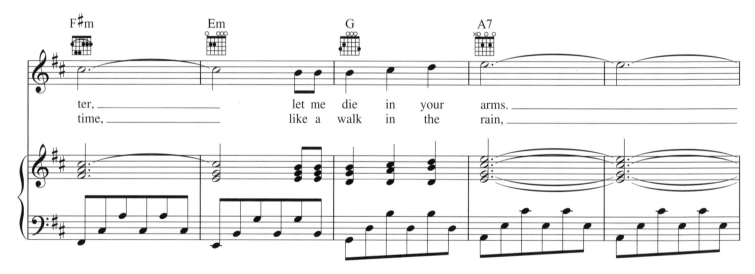

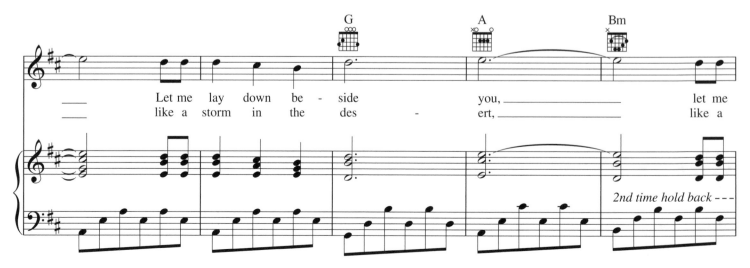

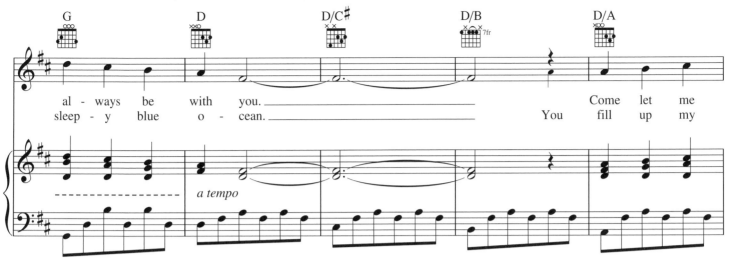

al - ways be with you. _____ Come let me
sleep - y blue o - cean. _____ You Come fill up my

------------------ *a tempo*

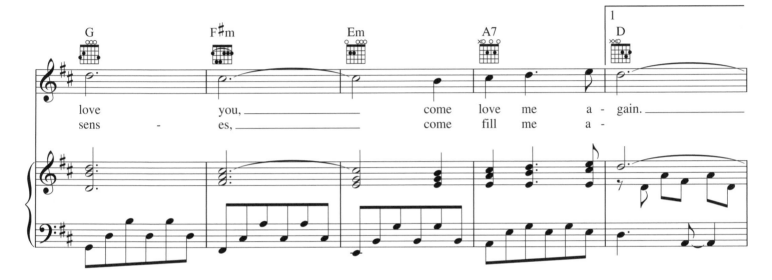

love you, _____ come love me a - gain. _____
sens - es, _____ come fill me a -

_____ You fill up my gain. _____

dim.

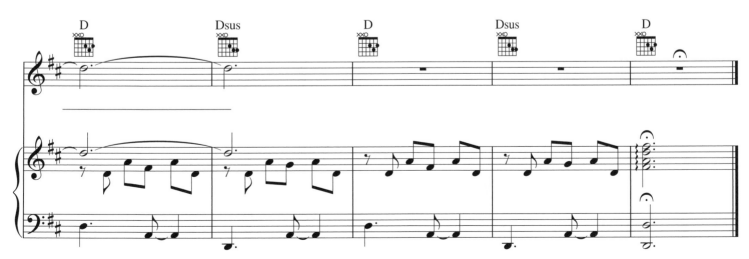

BEAUTIFUL IN MY EYES

Words and Music by
JOSHUA KADISON

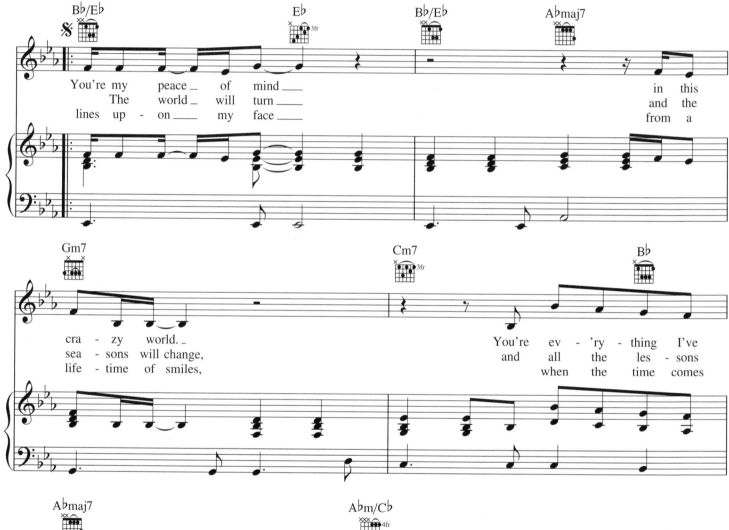

You're my peace __ of mind __ in this
The world __ will turn __ and the
lines up-on __ my face __ from a

cra — zy world. __ You're ev — 'ry — thing I've
sea — sons will change, and all the les — sons
life — time of smiles, when the time comes

tried to __ find. __ Your love __ is a pearl.
we will __ learn __ will be beau — ti — ful and strange. __
to em — brace __ for one __ long last while, __

D.S. al Coda
(take 2nd ending)

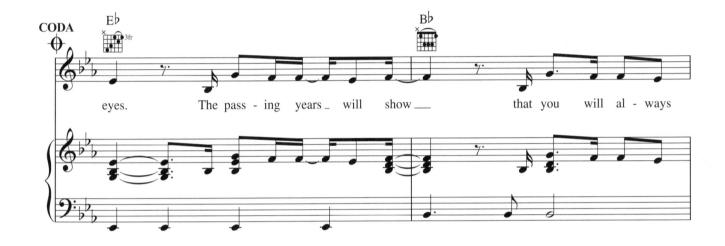

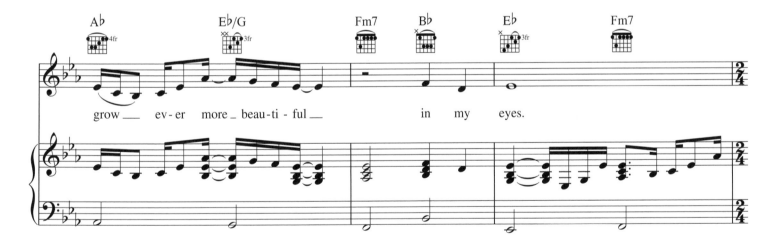

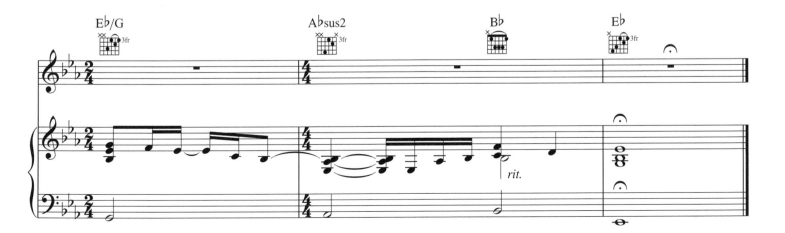

DON'T KNOW MUCH

Words and Music by BARRY MANN,
CYNTHIA WEIL and TOM SNOW

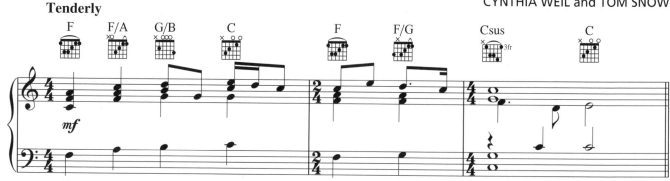

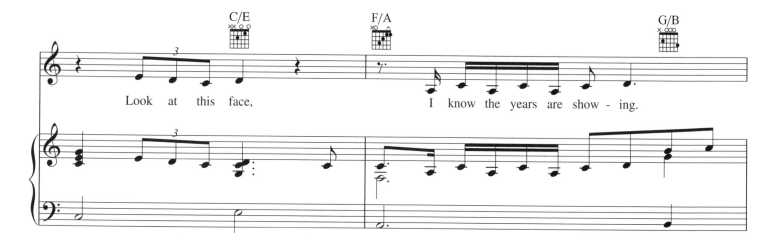

Look at this face, I know the years are show-ing.

Look at this life, _____ I still don't know where _ it's go-ing.

I don't know _ much, but I know I love you, _____ and

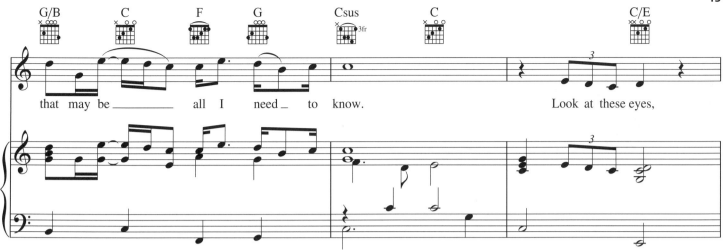

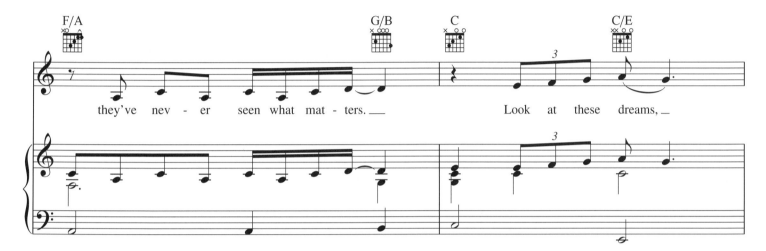

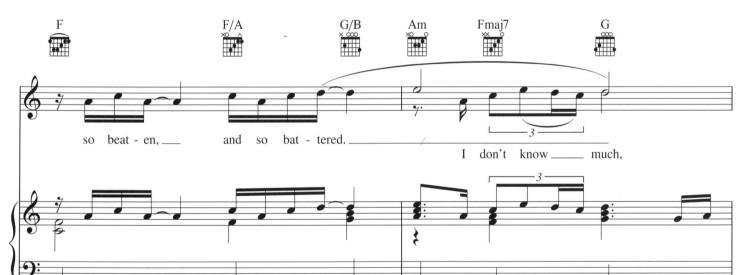

that may be ___ all I need ___ to know.

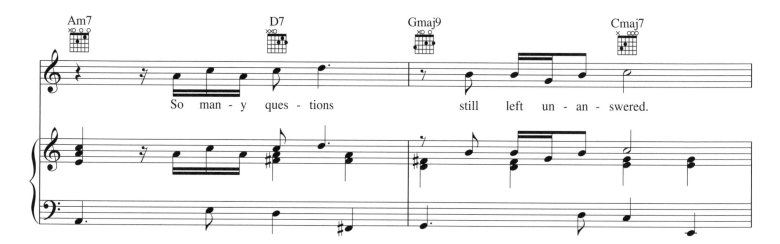

So man-y ques-tions still left un-an-swered.

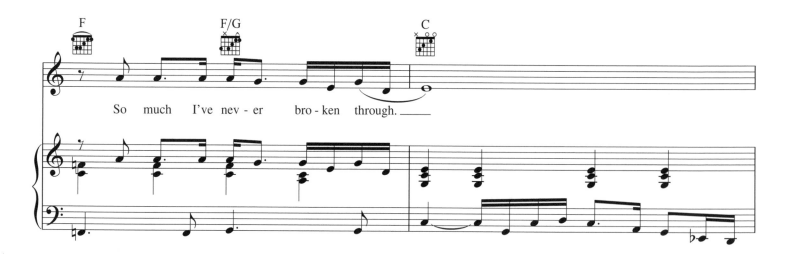

So much I've nev-er bro-ken through. ___

But when I feel you near me, some-times I see so clear-ly.

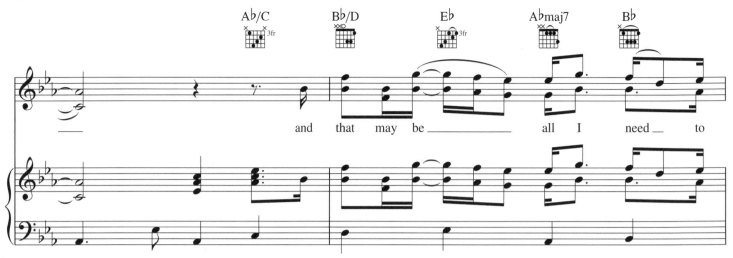

and that may be _____ all I need _ to

know.

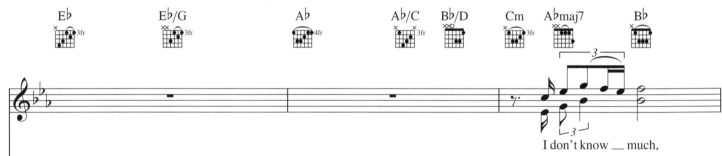

I don't know _ much,

but I know I love you, _____ and

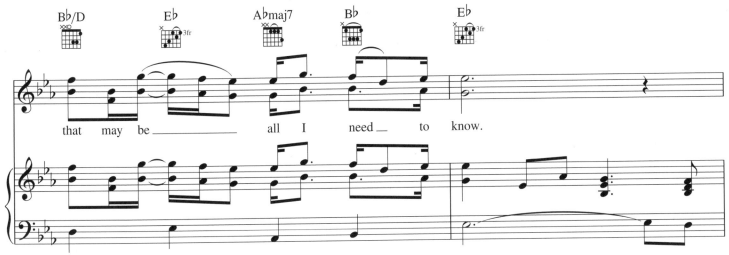

that may be ___ all I need ___ to know.

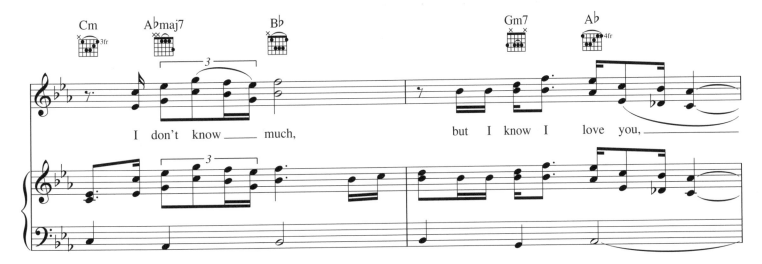

I don't know ___ much, but I know I love you, ___

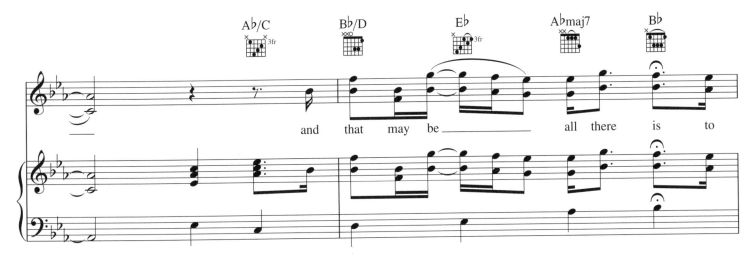

and that may be ___ all there is to

know. ___ Whoa. ___

ENDLESS LOVE

from ENDLESS LOVE

Words and Music by
LIONEL RICHIE

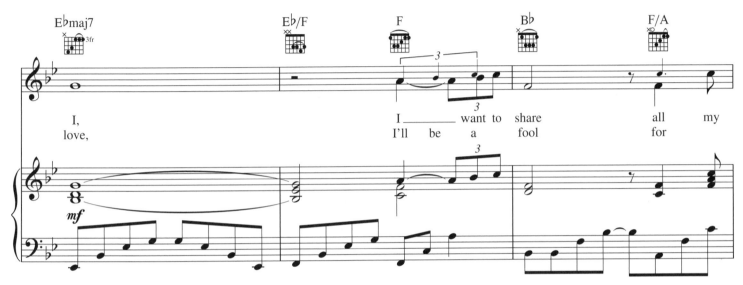

they tell me how much you care. ____ Oh, ____

you mean the world to ____ me. ____ Oh,

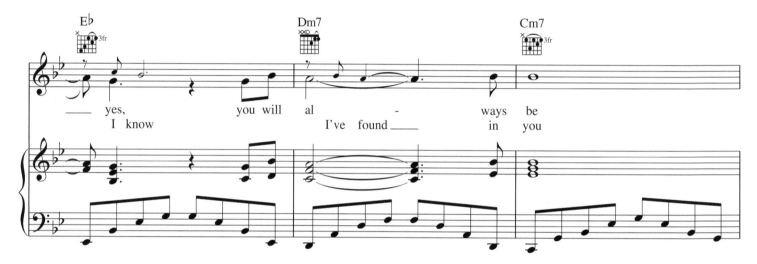

____ yes, you will al - ways be

I know I've found ____ in you

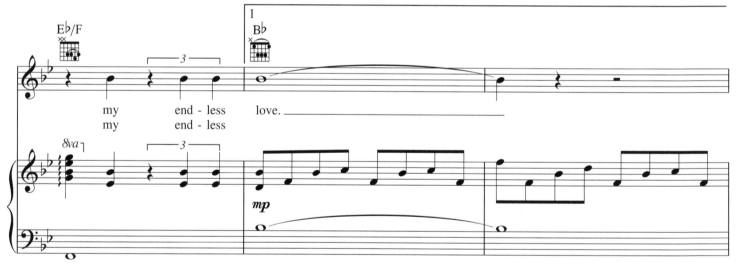

1

my end - less love. _____

my end - less

2

love. _____

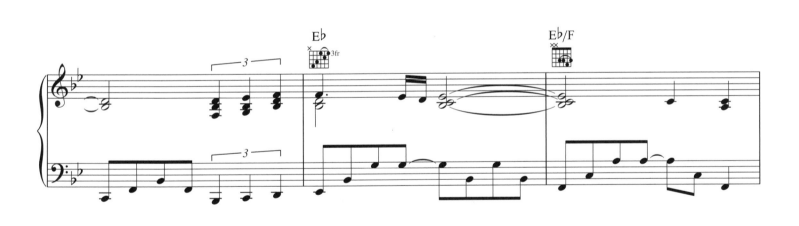

Oh, _____ and __ love, _____

cresc.

mf

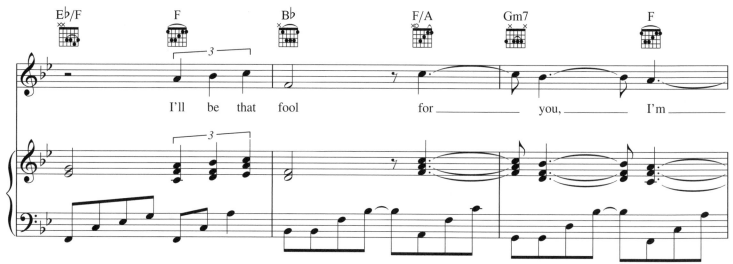

I'll be that fool for _____ you, _____ I'm

_____ sure; _____ you __ know I don't mind. _____

And yes, _____ you'll be the

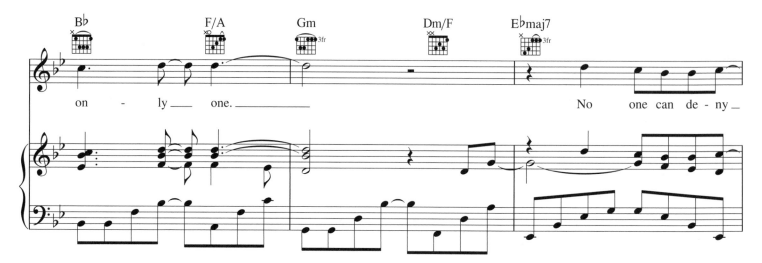

on - ly __ one. _____ No one can de - ny __

this love _____ I have in - side. I'll

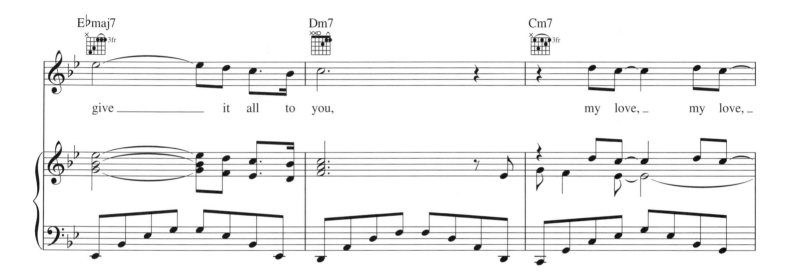

give _____ it all to you, my love, _ my love, _

_____ my end - less love.

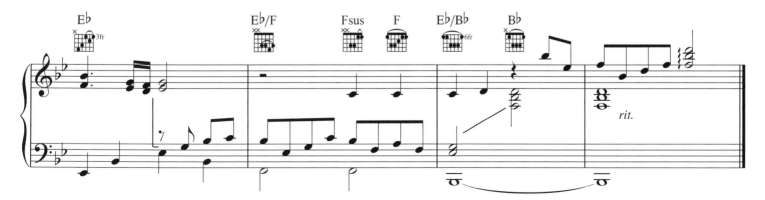

(Everything I Do)
I DO IT FOR YOU

from the Motion Picture ROBIN HOOD: PRINCE OF THIEVES

Words and Music by BRYAN ADAMS,
R.J. LANGE and MICHAEL KAMEN

you. There's no love like

your love, _____ and no oth - er could give

more _____ love. There's no _____ way, _____ un - less

you're _____ there all the time, _____ all the

way, __ yeah. _____

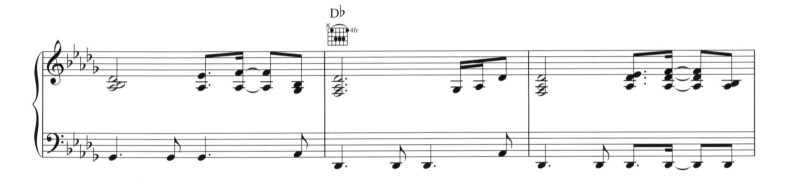

Oh, you can't tell me it's not worth try - ing for. I can't

Because You Loved Me

from UP CLOSE AND PERSONAL

Words and Music by
DIANE WARREN

For all ___ those times you stood ___ by me, for all ___ the
wings and made ___ me fly. You touched ___ my

truth that you made me see, for all ___ the joy you brought to my life, ___ for all ___ the
hand, I could touch the sky. I lost ___ my faith, you gave it back to me. You said ___ no

wrong that you ___ made right, for ev - 'ry ___ dream you made ___ come true, for all ___ the
star was out ___ of reach. You stood by ___ me and I ___ stood tall. I had ___ your

Recorded a half step lower.

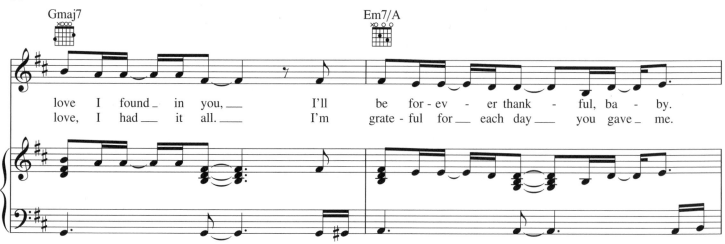

love I found_ in you, __ I'll be for - ev - er thank - ful, ba - by.
love, I had _ it all. __ I'm grate - ful for _ each day _ you gave _ me.

You're the one _ who held _ me up, nev - er let _ me fall. __
May - be I __ don't know _ that much, but I know this much _ is true. __

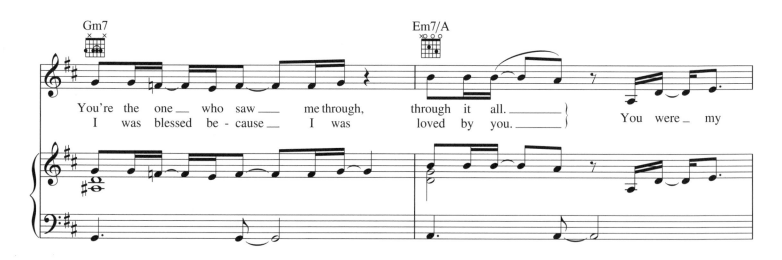

You're the one _ who saw __ me through, through it all. ____
I was blessed be - cause __ I was loved by you. ____ You were _ my

strength when I __ was weak. You were _ my voice when I could - n't speak. You were _ my

eyes when I could n't see. You saw __ the best there was __ in me, lift - ed __ me __

up when I could-n't reach. You gave __ me faith 'cause you __ be - lieved. __ I'm

ev-'ry-thing __ I am be-cause __ you loved __ me. You gave __ me

loved __ me. You were al - ways there __ for me, the ten-der wind __ that car - ried __ me, a

light in the dark, _ shin-ing your love _ in - to my _ life. _ You've

been my in - spi - ra - tion. _ Through the lies _ you were _ the truth. My

D.S. al Coda

world is a bet - ter place be - cause _ of you. _ You were _ my

CODA

loved _ me. You were _ my strength when I _ was weak. You were _ my

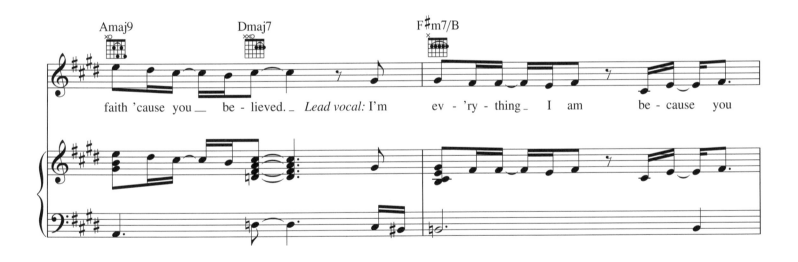

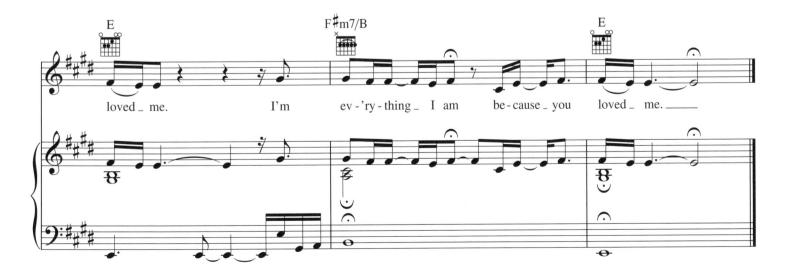

FAITHFULLY

Words and Music by
JONATHAN CAIN

Slow Rock

High - way,

run   in - to the mid - night   sun.
life   un - der the big - top   world;

Wheels go 'round   and 'round;   you're on my   mind.
we all need   the clowns   to make us   smile.

And lov-in' a mu-sic man__ ain't al-ways what it's
I get the joy__ of re - dis-

s'pposed to be.__ }
cov-'ring you.__ }

Oh girl, you stand__ by

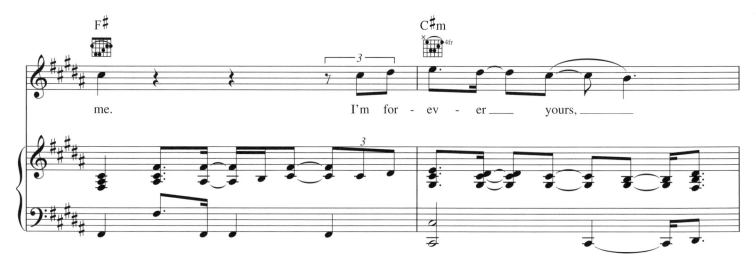

me. I'm for-ev-er__ yours,__

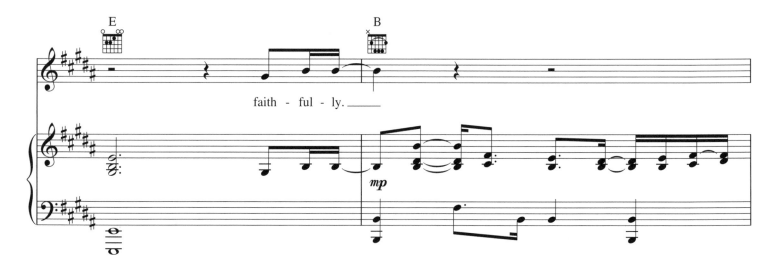

faith - ful - ly.__

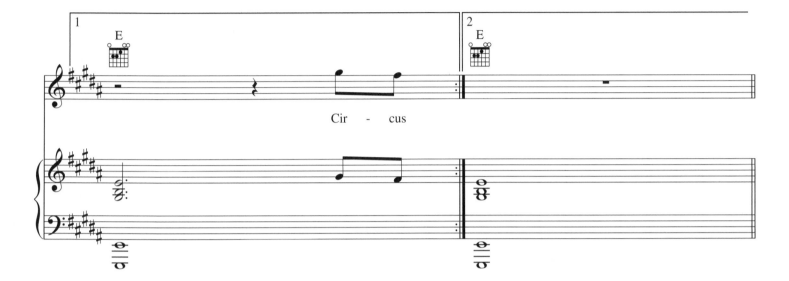

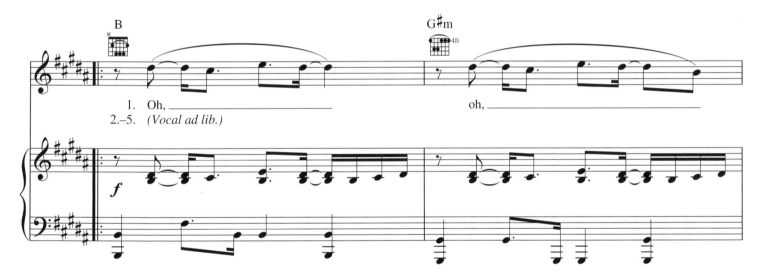

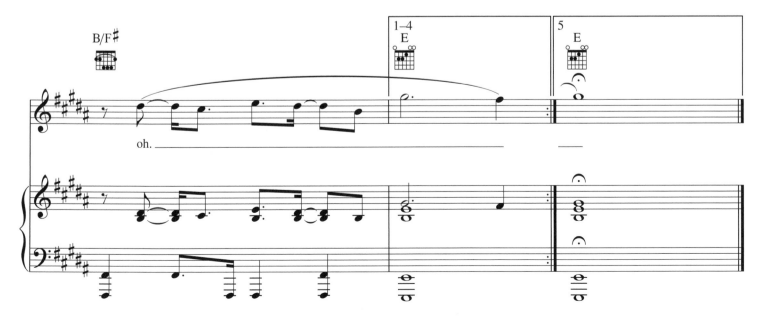

FOR THE FIRST TIME

from ONE FINE DAY

Words and Music by JAMES NEWTON HOWARD,
JUD FRIEDMAN and ALLAN RICH

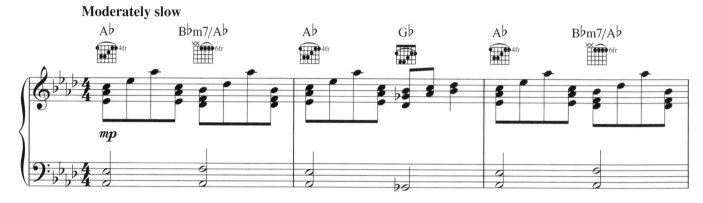

Are those your eyes? ___ real? Is ___ that your smile? Can ___ this be true? I've been Am I the

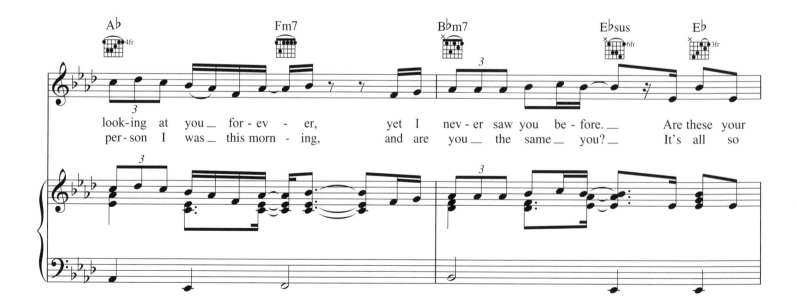

look-ing at you ___ for-ev-er, yet I nev-er saw you be-fore. ___ Are these your
per-son I was ___ this morn - ing, and are you ___ the same ___ you? ___ It's all so

how much __ I see __ when you're look-ing back __ at me. _____ Now I

un - der - stand __ what love is, ___ love ___ is for the first __

__ time. __ Can this be __ time. __

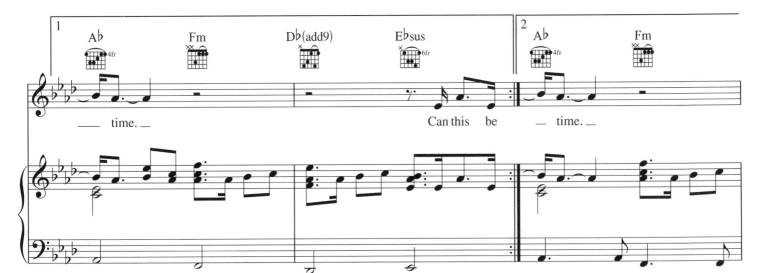

Such a long time __ a - go, I had

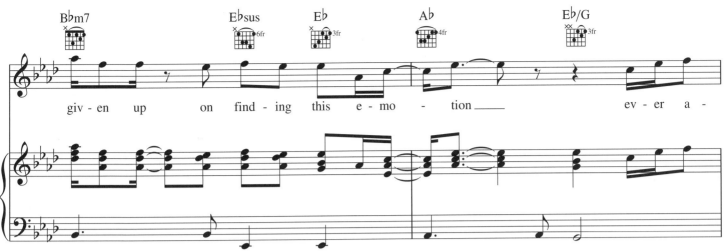

giv - en up on find - ing this e - mo - tion ____ ev - er a -

gain. ____ But you're here with me now. ____ Yes, I

found you some - how, _ and I've nev - er been ___ so sure. ___

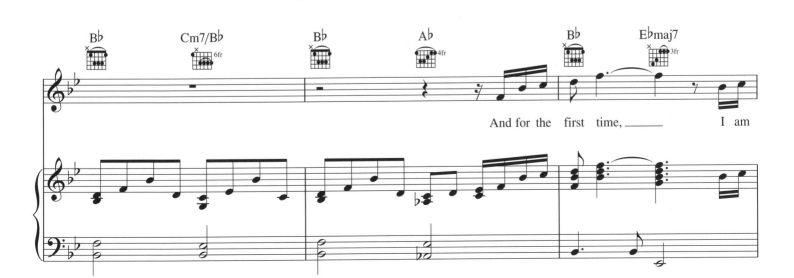

And for the first time, _____ I am

HAVE I TOLD YOU LATELY

Words and Music by
VAN MORRISON

Slowly, with expression

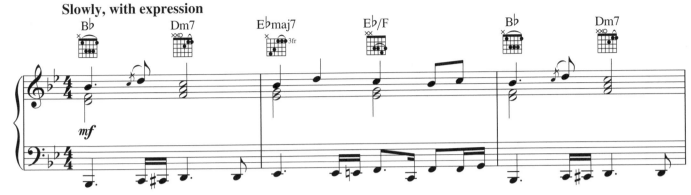

Have I told ___ you late-ly that I love you? Have I

told you there's no one else ___ a-bove ___ you?

Fill my heart ___ with glad-ness, take a-way all ___ my sad-ness,

ease my trou-bles, that's __ what you do.

(For the
Instrumental solo

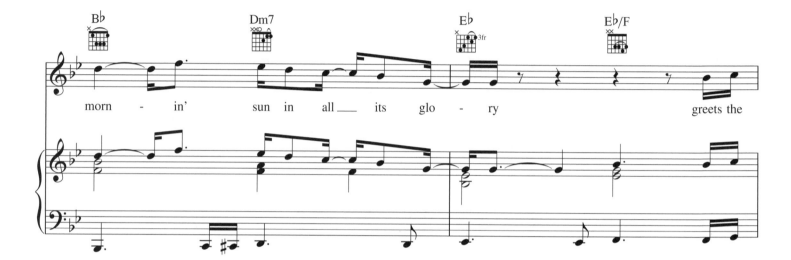

morn - in' sun in all __ its glo - ry

greets the

day with hope and com-fort, too. ___

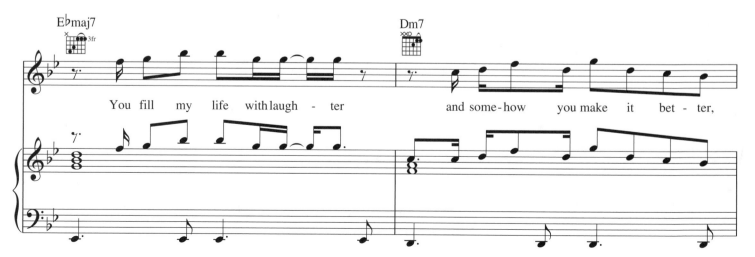

You fill my life with laugh - ter

and some-how you make it bet - ter,

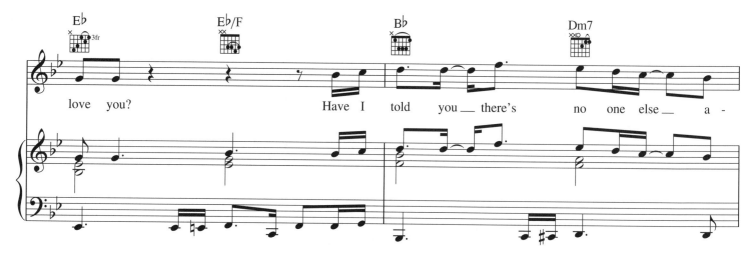

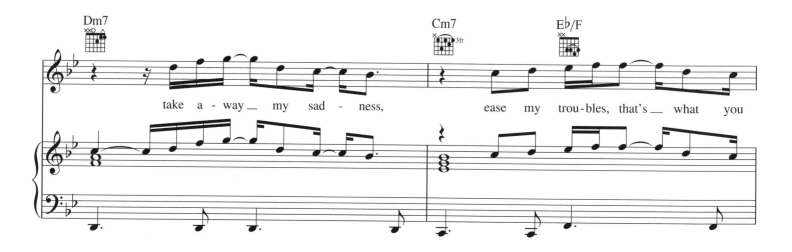

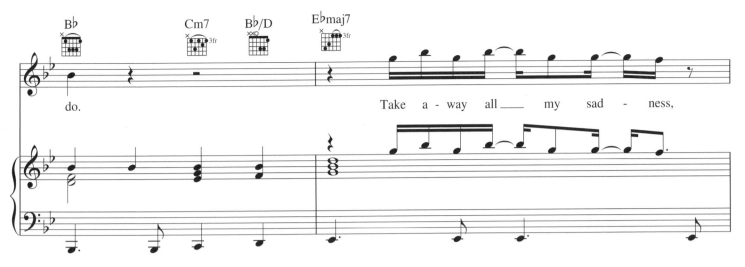

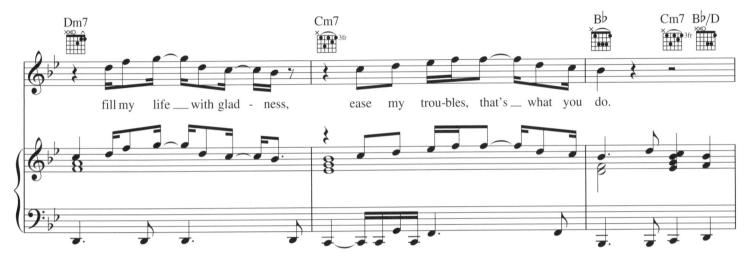

FRIENDS

Words and Music by MICHAEL W. SMITH
and DEBORAH D. SMITH

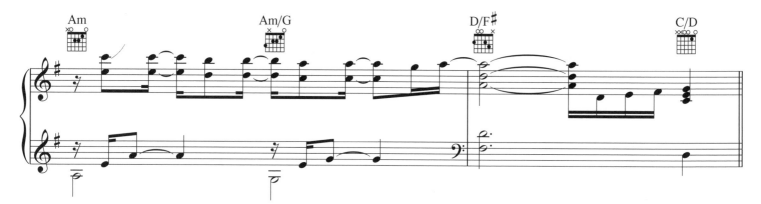

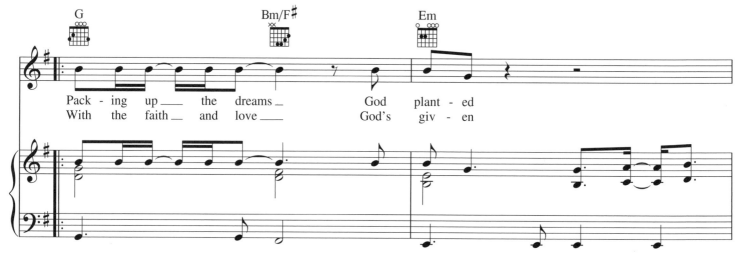

Pack-ing up ___ the dreams ___ God plant-ed
With the faith ___ and love ___ God's giv-en

in the fer-tile soil ___ of ___ you,
spring-ing from ___ the hope ___ we ___ know,

can't be - lieve __ the hopes __ He's grant - ed means a
we will pray __ the joy __ you'll live in

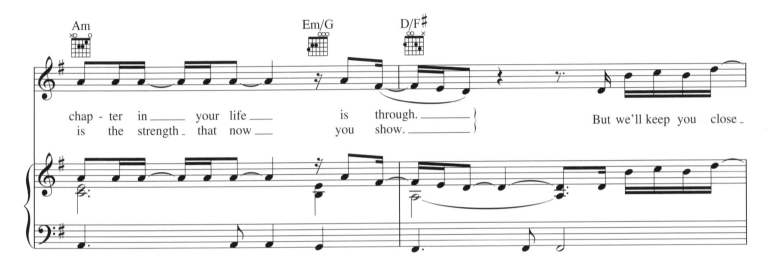

chap - ter in _____ your life _____ is through. _____ But we'll keep you close __
is the strength __ that now __ you show. _____

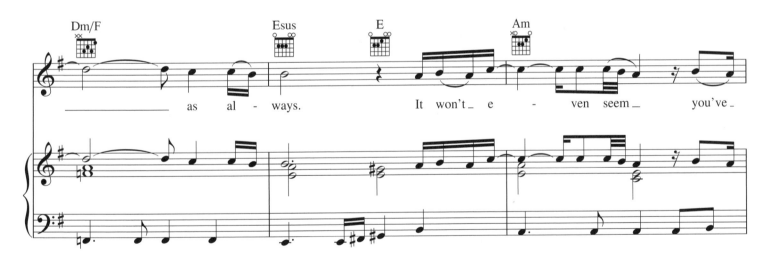

_____ as al - ways. It won't __ e - ven seem __ you've __

gone. 'Cause our hearts __ in big _____ and small __ ways __ will

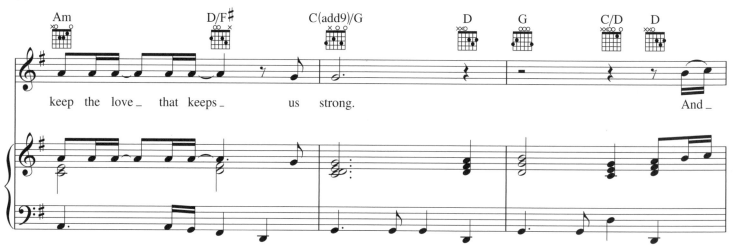

keep the love _ that keeps _ us strong. And _

friends are friends _ for - ev - er if the Lord's the Lord _ of them, _ and a

friend will not _ say "nev - er" 'cause the wel - come will _ not end. _ Though it's

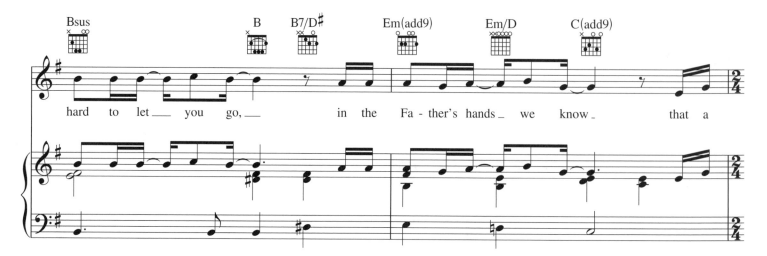

hard to let _ you go, _ in the Fa - ther's hands _ we know _ that a

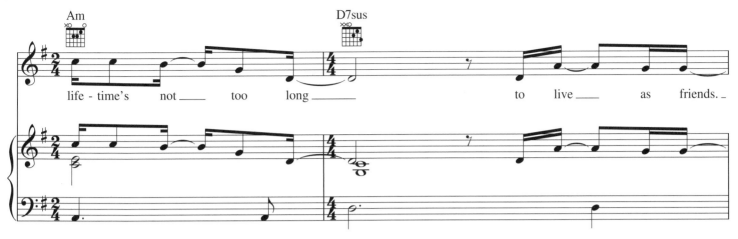

life-time's not ____ too long ____ to live ____ as friends. ____

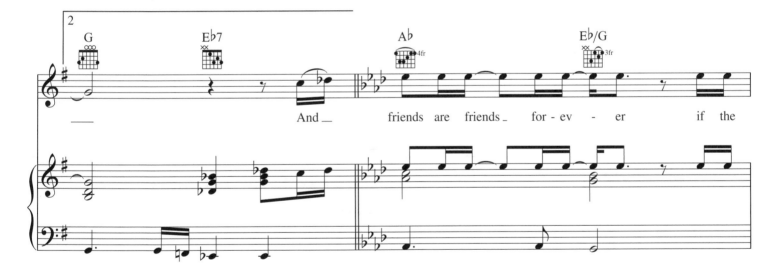

And ____ friends are friends ____ for-ev-er ____ if the

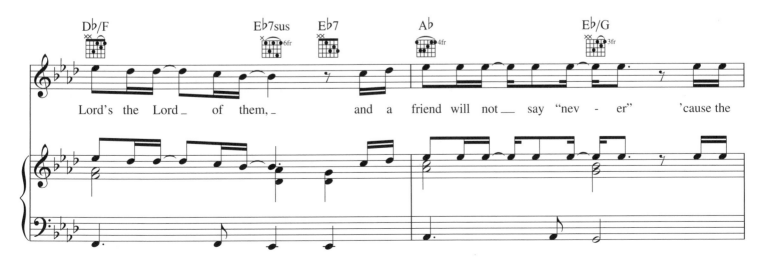

Lord's the Lord ____ of them, ____ and a friend will not ____ say "nev-er" ____ 'cause the

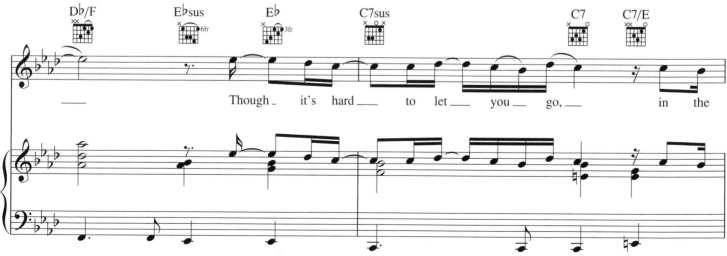

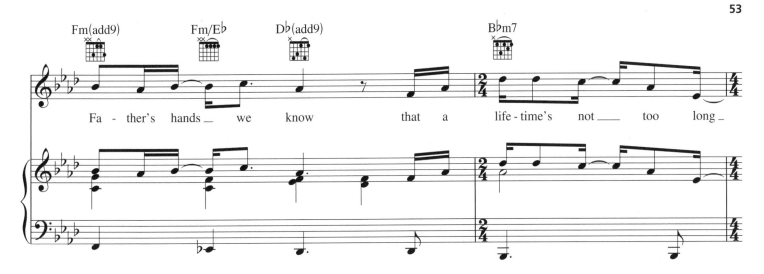

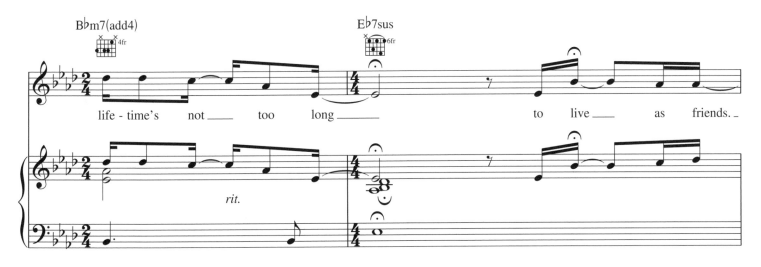

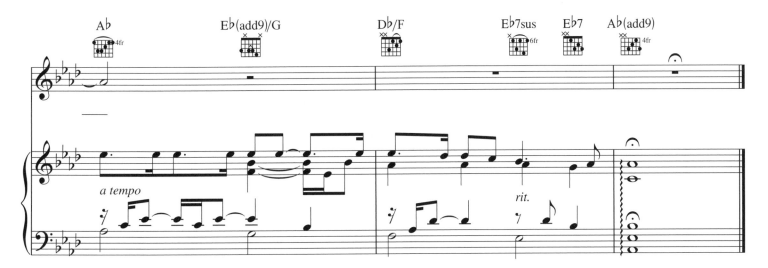

HELLO

Words and Music by
LIONEL RICHIE

Slow Ballad

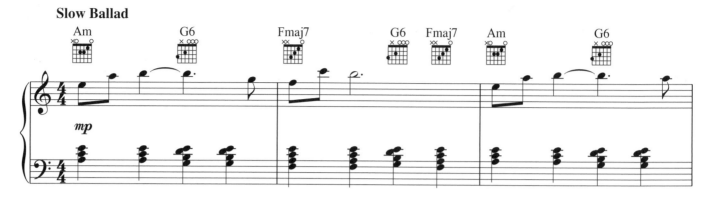

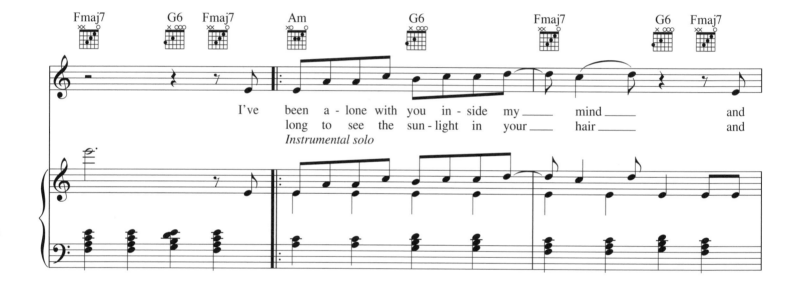

I've been a-lone with you in-side my _____ mind _____ and
long to see the sun-light in your _____ hair _____ and
Instrumental solo

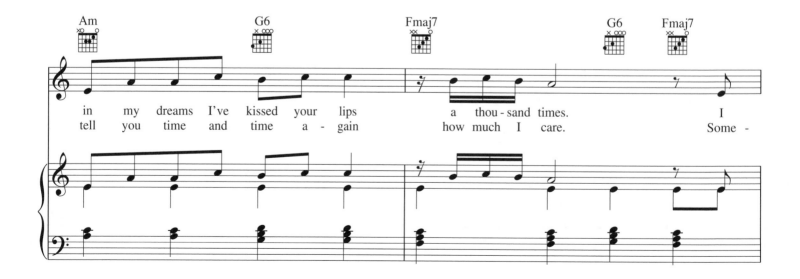

in my dreams I've kissed your lips a thou-sand times. I
tell you time and time a-gain how much I care. Some-

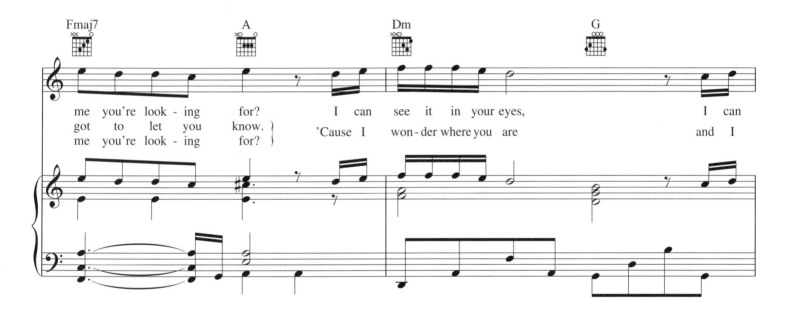

I WILL ALWAYS LOVE YOU

featured in THE BODYGUARD

Words and Music by
DOLLY PARTON

will_ al - ways_ love_ you. _____ I _____

D.S.

___ will_ al - ways_ love_ you. _____

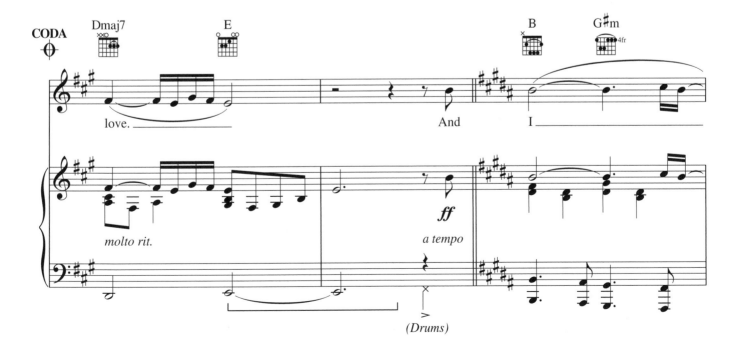

CODA

love. _____ And I _____

molto rit.

ff

a tempo

(Drums)

will al - ways love you. I will al - ways love

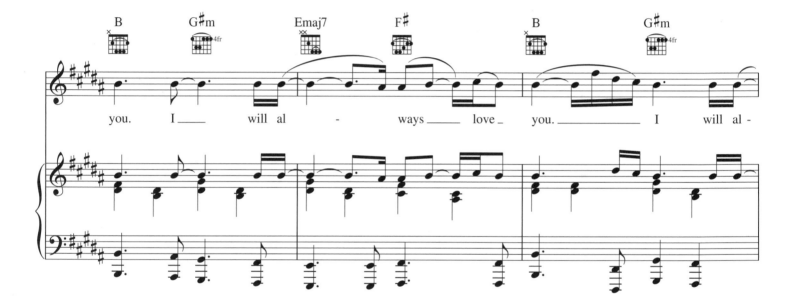

you. I will al - ways love you. I will al -

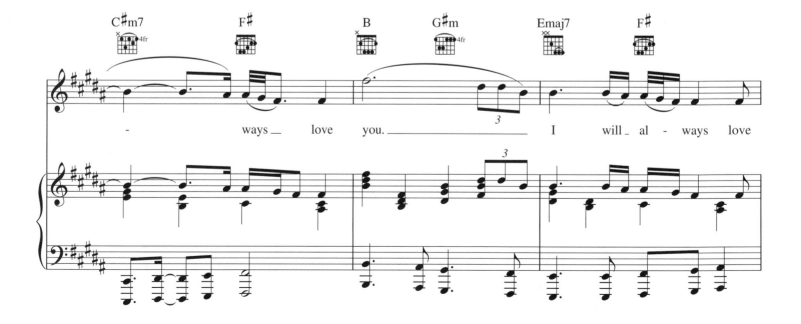

- ways love you. I will al - ways love

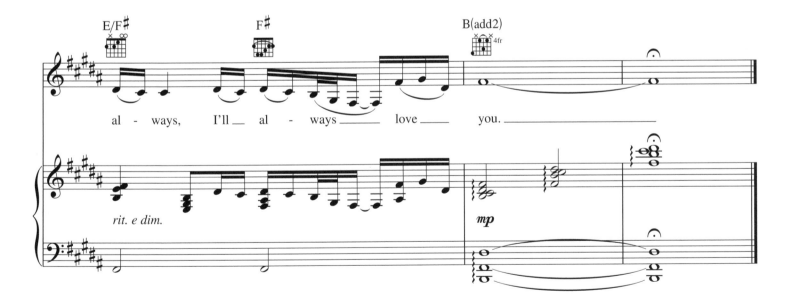

Additional Lyrics

3. I hope life treats you kind.
And I hope you have all you've dreamed of.
And I wish to you, joy and happiness.
But above all this, I wish you love.

I JUST CALLED TO SAY I LOVE YOU

Words and Music by
STEVIE WONDER

Chorus

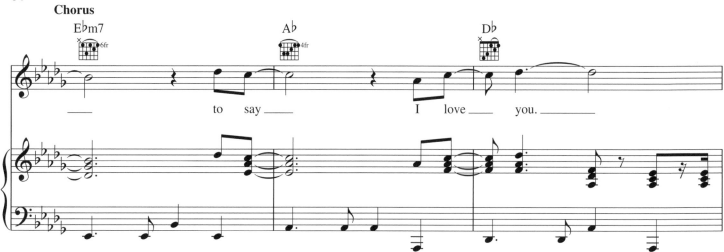

to say ___ I love ___ you. ___

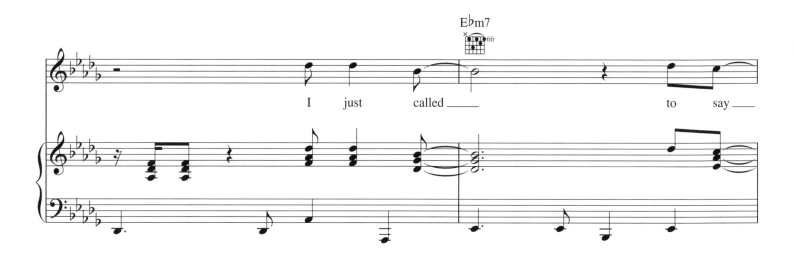

I just called ___ to say ___

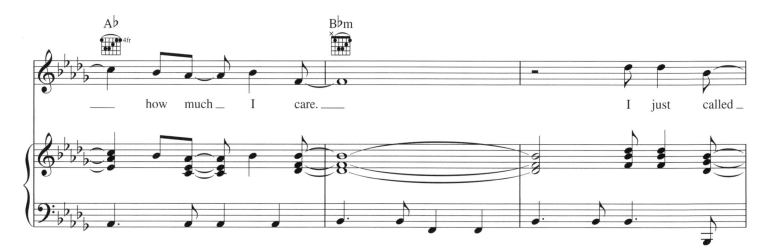

___ how much ___ I care. ___ I just called ___

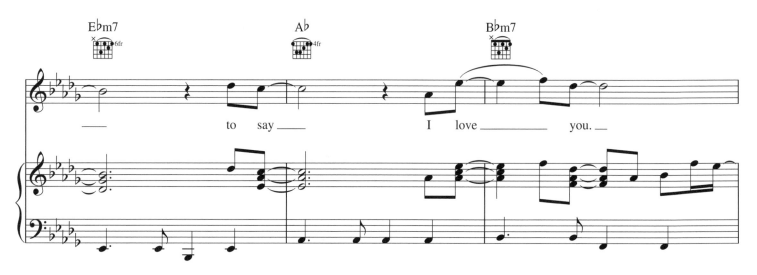

___ to say ___ I love ___ you. ___

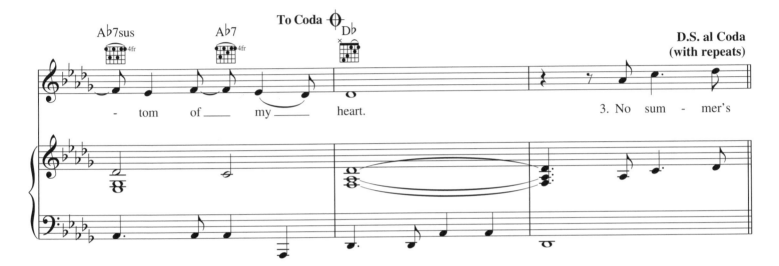

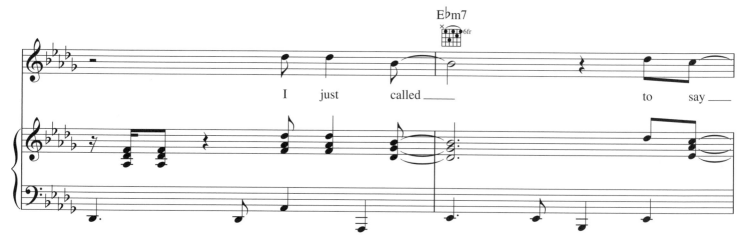

I just called _____ to say _____

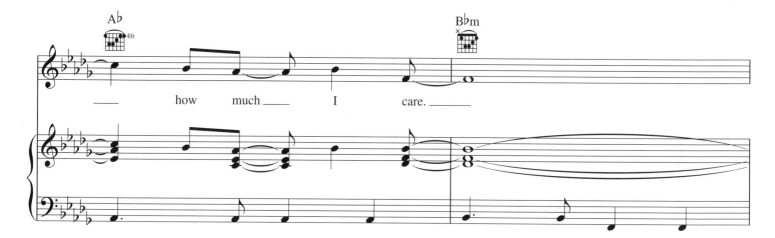

_____ how much _____ I care. _____

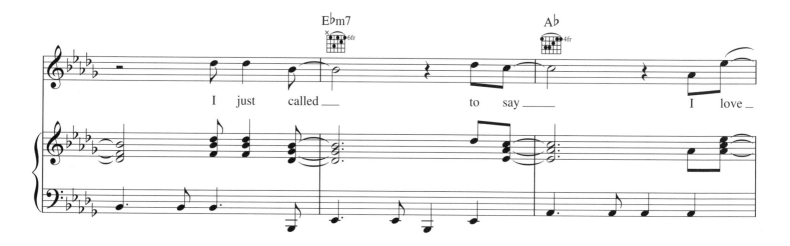

I just called _____ to say _____ I love _

_____ you. _ And I mean _ it from _ the bot -

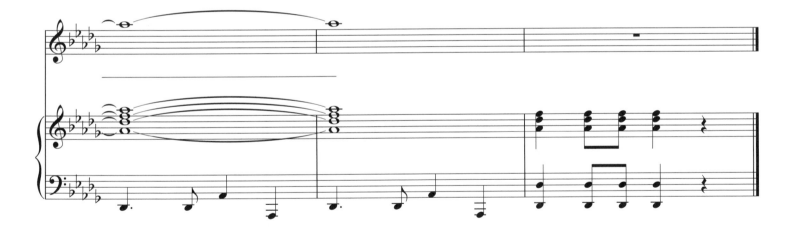

Additional Lyrics

3. No summer's high; no warm July;
   No harvest moon to light one tender August night.
   No autumn breeze; no falling leaves;
   Not even time for birds to fly to southern skies.

4. No Libra sun; no Halloween;
   No giving thanks to all the Christmas joy you bring.
   But what it is, though old so new
   To fill your heart like no three words could ever do.
   Chorus

I WILL BE HERE

Words and Music by
STEVEN CURTIS CHAPMAN

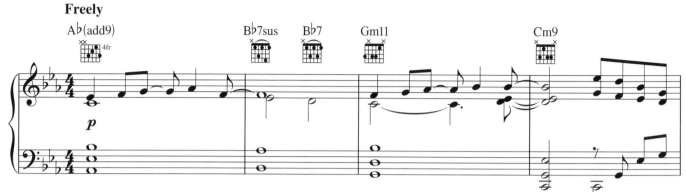

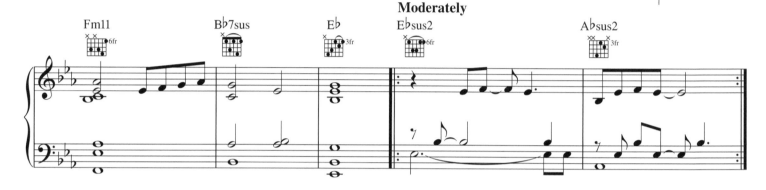

To-mor-row morn-in' if you ___ wake up and the sun does not ___ ap-pear, ___
To-mor-row morn-in' if you ___ wake up and the fu-ture is ___ un-clear, ___

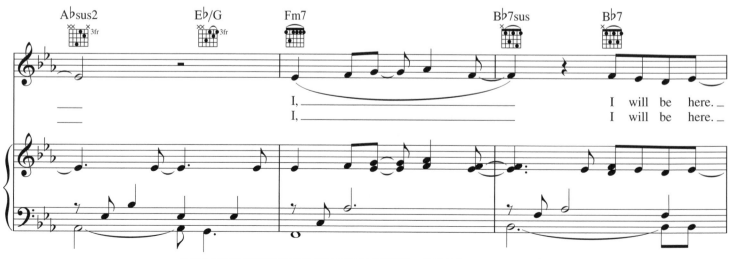

___ I, _____ I will be here. ___
___ I, _____ I will be here. ___

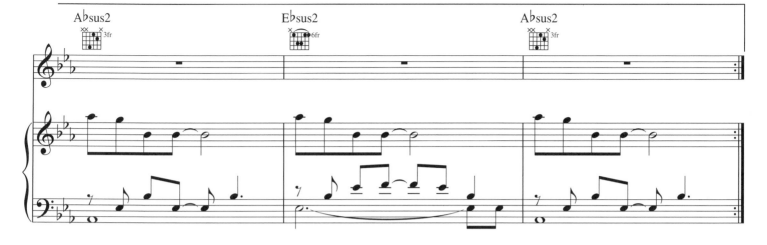

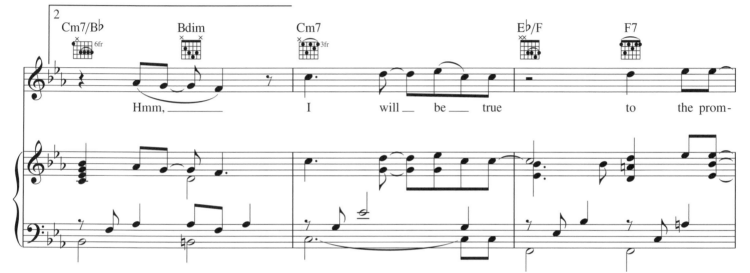

Hmm, _____ I will ___ be ___ true to the prom-

- ise I ___ have _____ made to you and to _____ the One ___

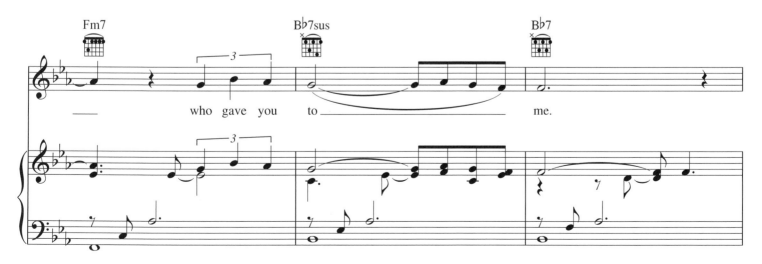

___ who gave you to _____ me.

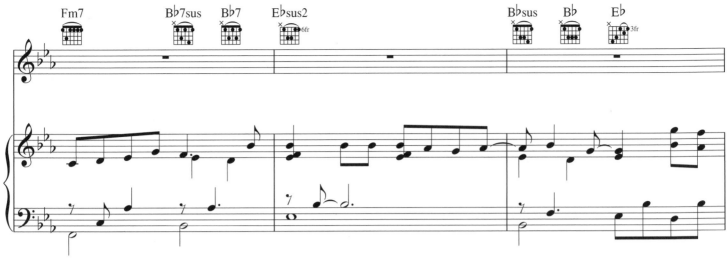

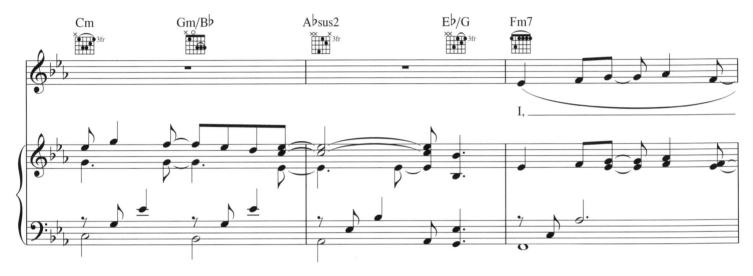

I,

I will be here. ___ And _____ just as sure as sea-sons are made ___ for ___ change, ___ our life-times are made ___ for ___

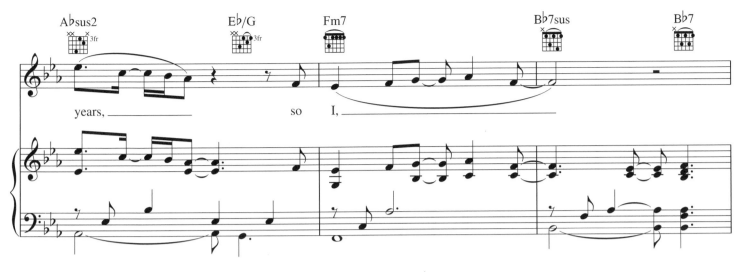

years, _____ so I, _____

I _____ will be _____ here. _____ We'll be to - geth - er. ____

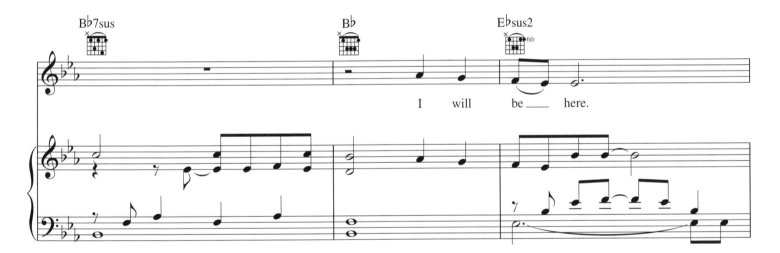

I will be _____ here.

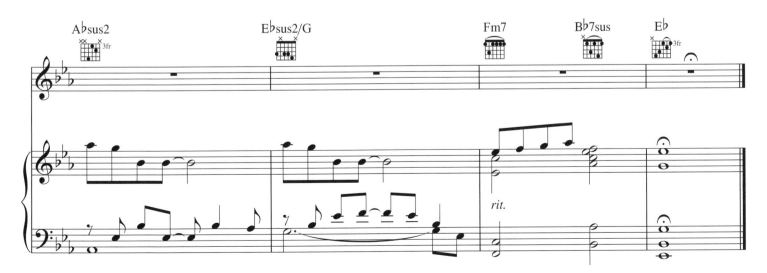

rit.

I'LL BE

Words and Music by
EDWIN McCAIN

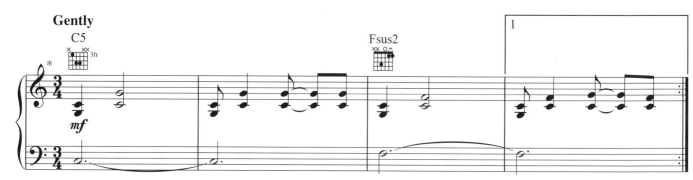

The strands in your eyes ___ that col - or them ___
rain falls ___ an - gry on the

won - der - ful ___ stop me ___ and steal my ___ breath. ___
tin roof as ___ we lie ___ a - wake in my bed. ___

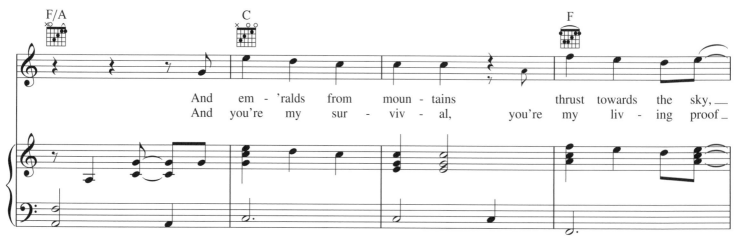

And em - 'ralds from moun - tains thrust towards the sky,
And you're my sur - vi - val, you're my liv - ing proof ___

*Recorded a half step lower.

nev - er re - veal - ing their __ depth. __
my love is a - live and not __ dead. __

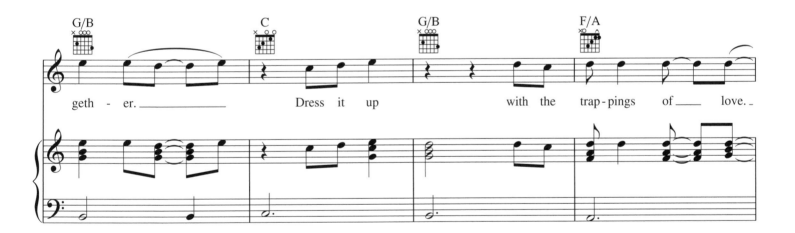

And tell __ me that we be - long __ to -

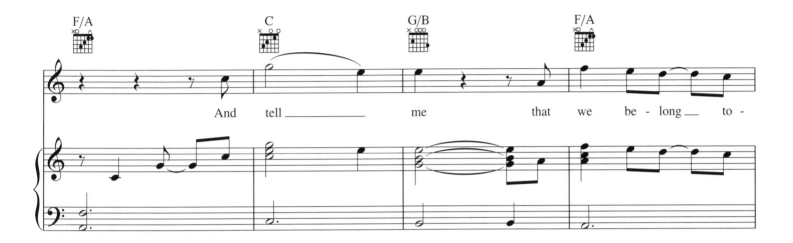

geth - er. __ Dress it up with the trap - pings of __ love. __

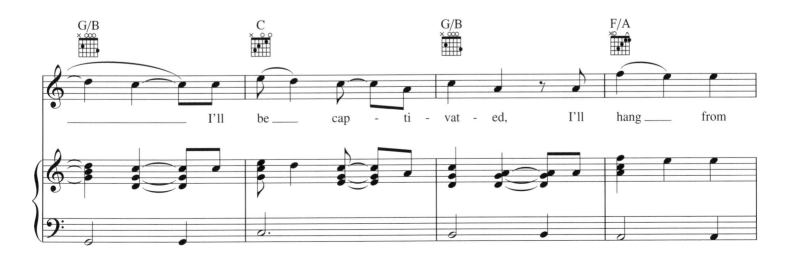

__ I'll be cap - ti - vat - ed, I'll hang __ from

your — lips in - stead of — the — gal - lows of heart - ache — that

hang from a - bove. _____

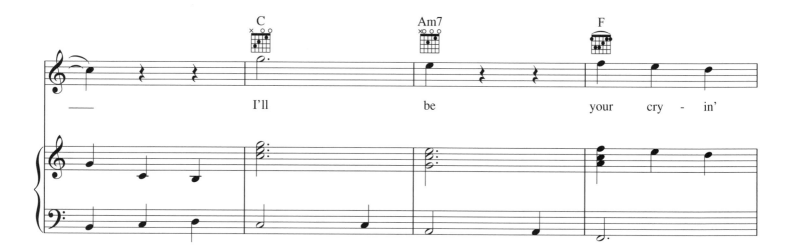

— I'll be your cry - in'

shoul - der, _____ I'll — be _____ love su - i - cide. _____

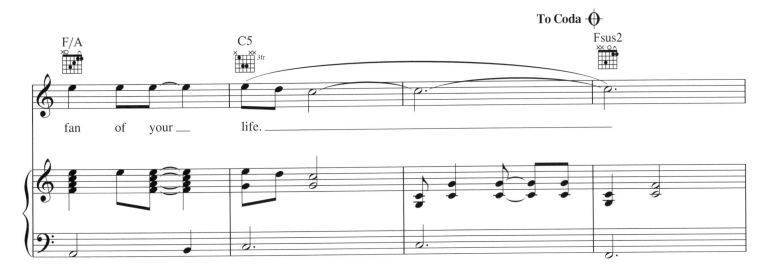

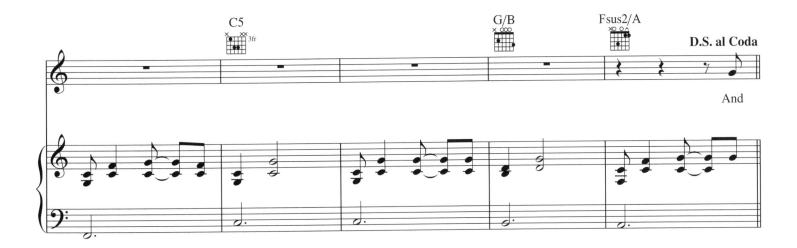

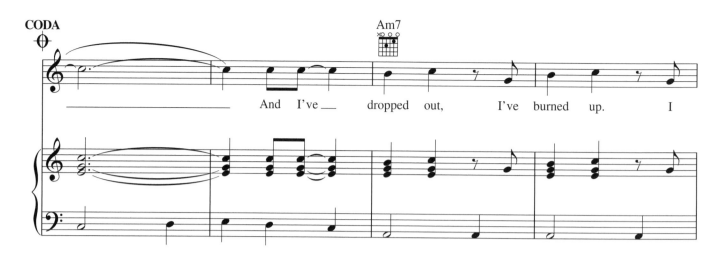

And I've ___ dropped out, I've burned up. I

fought my way back from the dead. ___

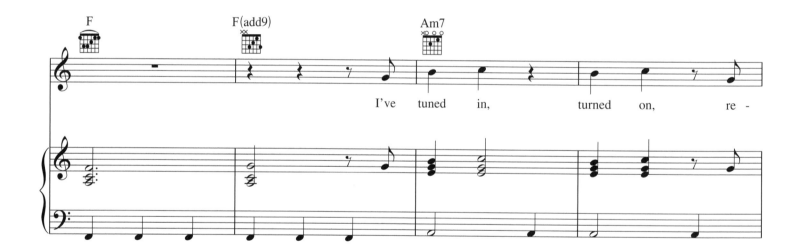

I've tuned in, turned on, re -

mem - bered ___ the thing that you said. ___

I'll   be

your cry - in' shoul - der,_____   I'll_____ be_____   love

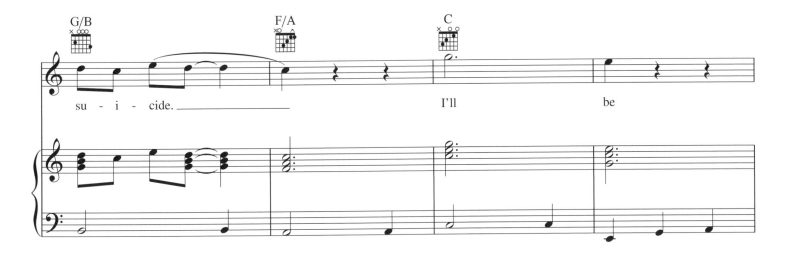

su - i - cide._____   I'll   be

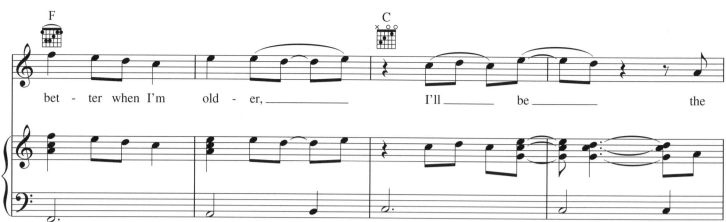

bet - ter when I'm old - er, _____ I'll _____ be _____ the

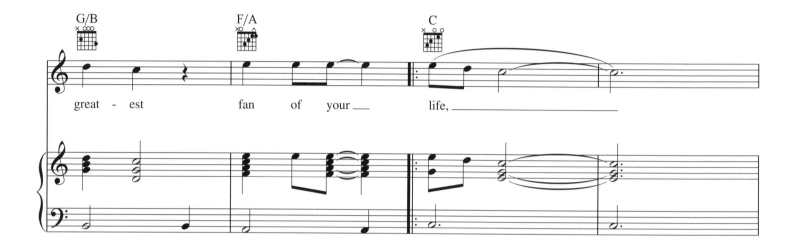

great - est fan of your ___ life, _____

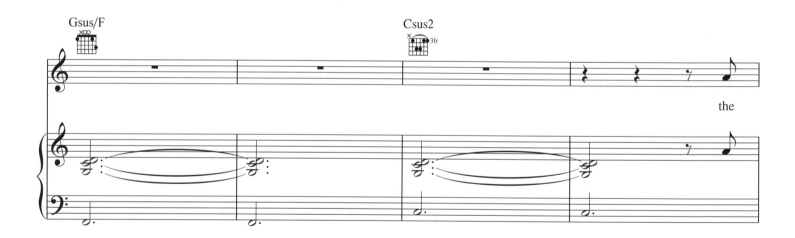

the

Repeat and Fade **Optional Ending**

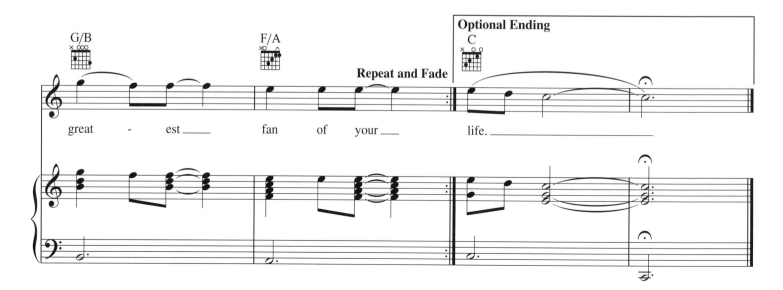

great - est _____ fan of your ___ life. _____

IN MY LIFE

Words and Music by JOHN LENNON
and PAUL McCARTNEY

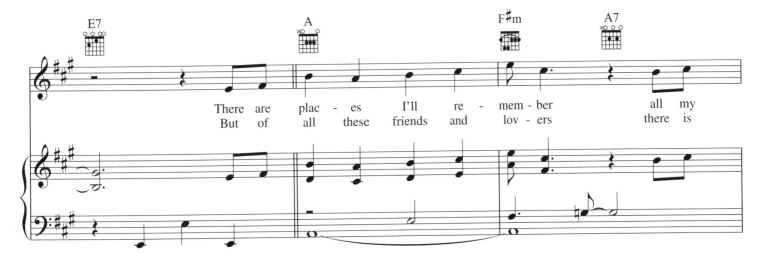

There are plac - es I'll re - mem - ber all my
But of all these friends and lov - ers there is

life, _____ though some have changed. _ Some for - ev - er, not for
no _____ one com - pares with you. _ And these mem - 'ries lose their

bet - ter; some have gone _____ and some re - main. _ All these
mean - ing when I think of _ love as some - thing new. _ Tho' I

(1.) plac - es ___ had ___ their ___ mo - ments / with lov - ers and friends ___ I
(2.,3.) know ___ I'll ___ nev - er lose af - fec - tion / for peo - ple and things ___ that

still can re - call. ___ Some are dead ___ and ___ some ___ are
went ___ be - fore, ___ I know I'll of - ten stop and think a -

liv - ing, ___ in my ___ life I've loved them all. ___
bout them, ___ in my ___ life I love you more. ___

In 18th century style

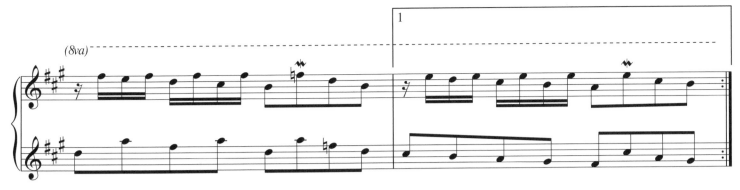

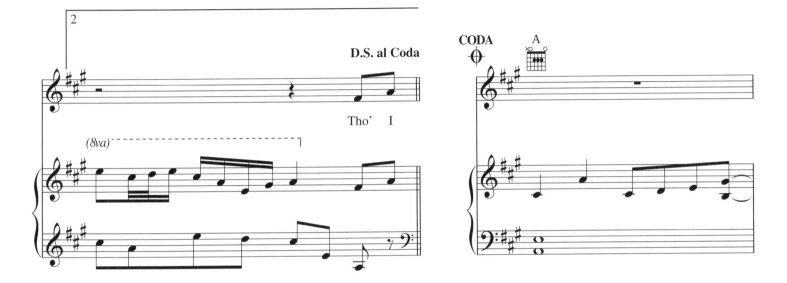

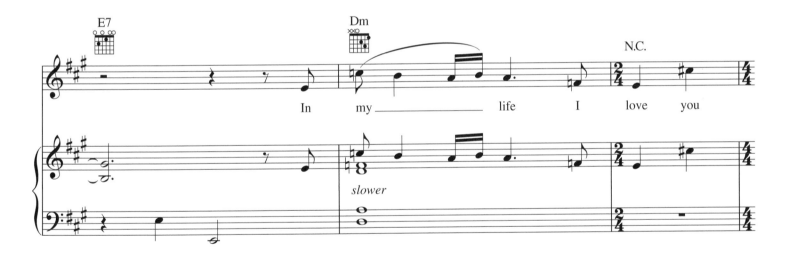

IF

Words and Music by
DAVID GATES

Moderately, with feeling

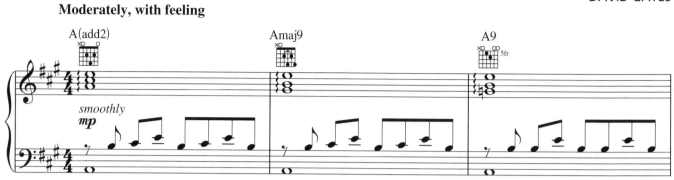

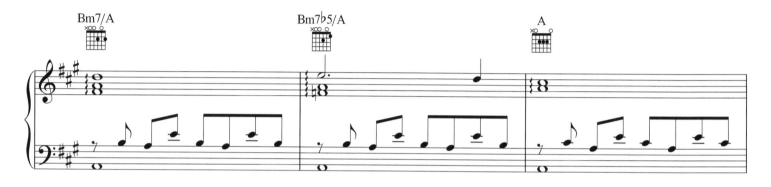

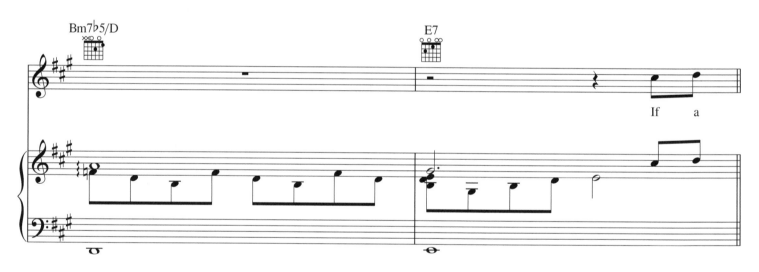

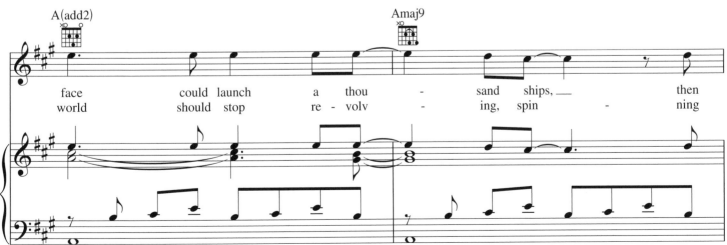

I'LL HAVE TO SAY I LOVE YOU IN A SONG

Words and Music by
JIM CROCE

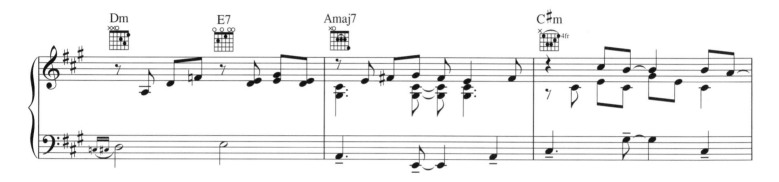

Well, I know it's kind of late. ___
know it's kind of strange ___

Instrumental solo

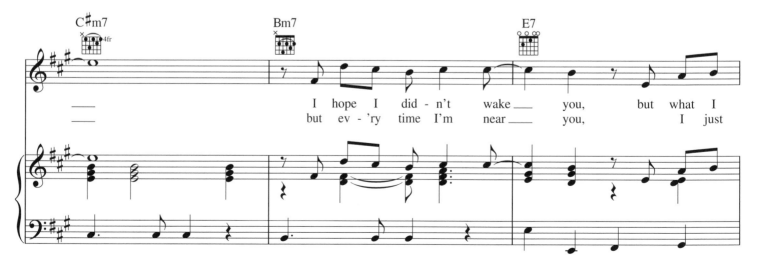

___ I hope I did - n't wake ___ you, but what I
___ but ev - 'ry time I'm near ___ you, I just

got to say can't wait. ___
run out of things to say. ___

I know you'd un-der-stand. ___
I know you'd un-der-stand. ___

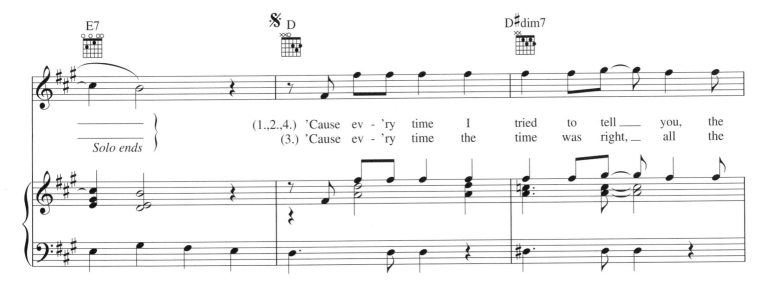

Solo ends

(1.,2.,4.) 'Cause ev-'ry time I tried to tell ___ you, the
(3.) 'Cause ev-'ry time the time was right, ___ all the

words just came out wrong. ___
words just came out wrong. ___

So I'll have to say ___ I love ___
So I'll have to say ___ I love ___

To Coda

___ you in a song. ___
___ you in a song. ___

Yeah, I
Instrumental solo

some-thin' that I just got to say. ___ I know you'd un - der - stand. ___

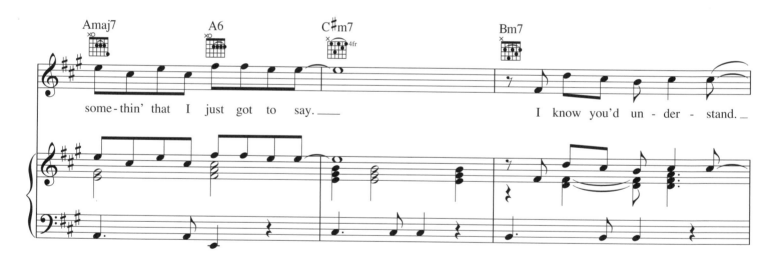

D.S. al Coda

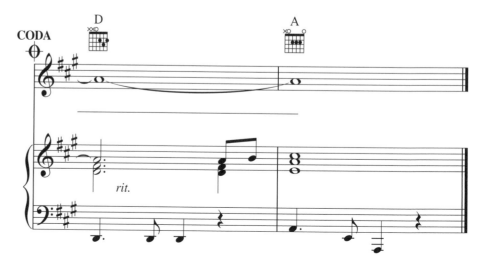

CODA

rit.

JUST THE WAY YOU ARE

Words and Music by
BILLY JOEL

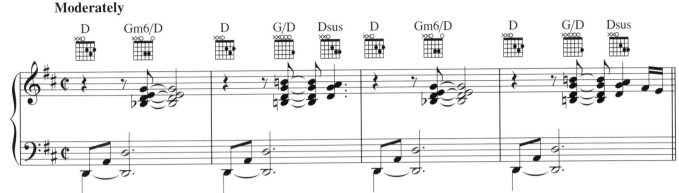

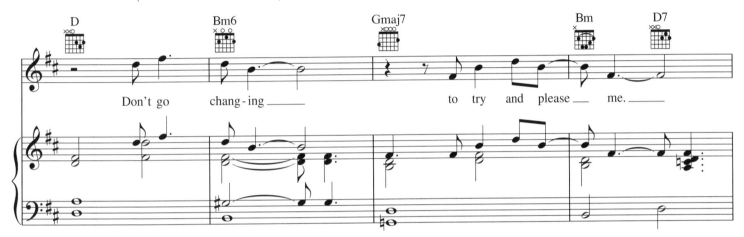

Don't go chang-ing _____ to try and please _ me. _____

You nev- er let me down _ be - fore. _____ Mm, _____ mm. _____

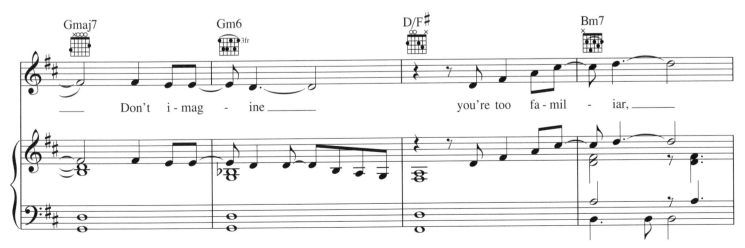

_____ Don't i-mag - ine _____ you're too fa - mil - iar, _____

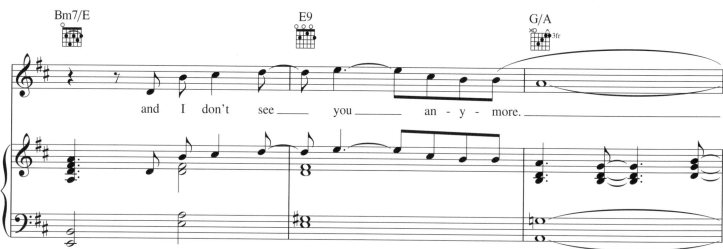

and I don't see ___ you ___ an - y - more. ___

___ I _____ would __ not leave you ___

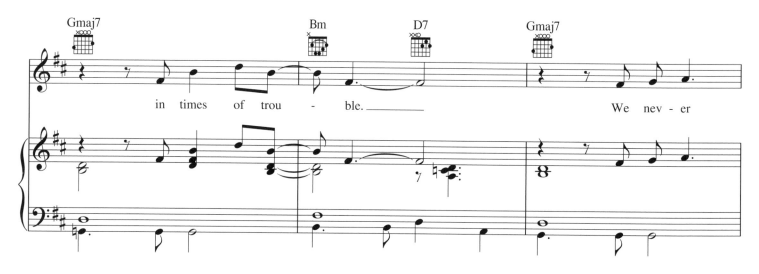

in times of trou - ble. _____ We nev - er

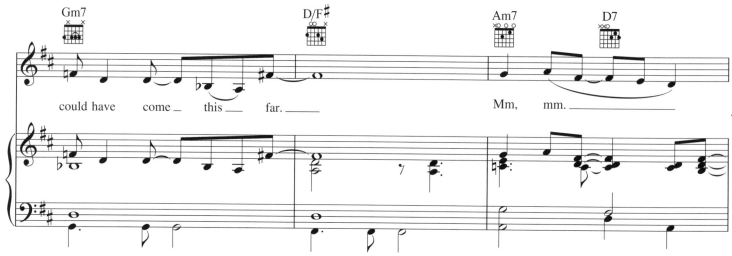

could have come __ this __ far. ___ Mm, mm. _____

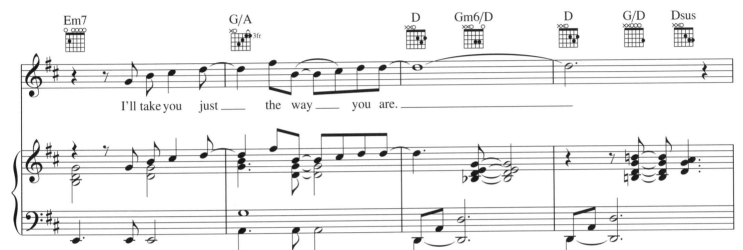

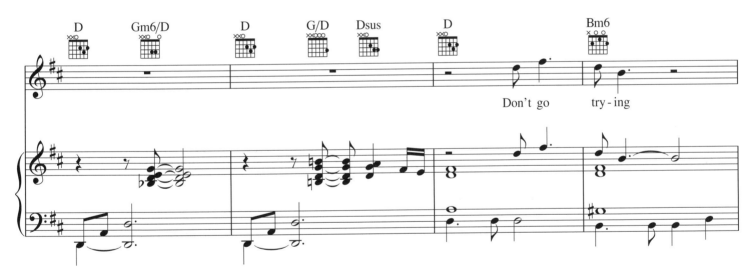

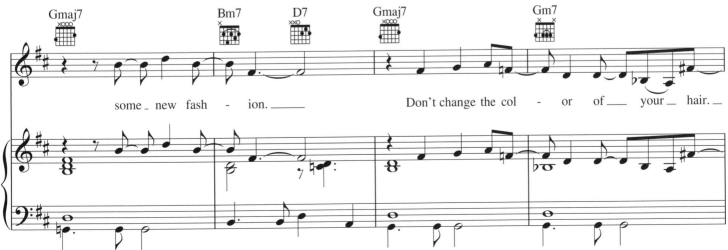

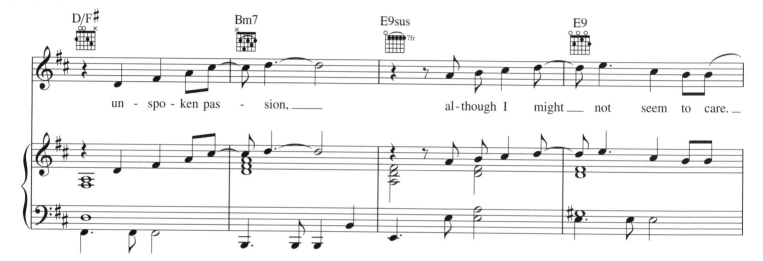

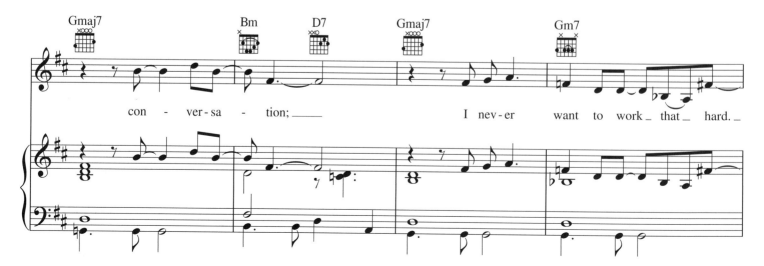

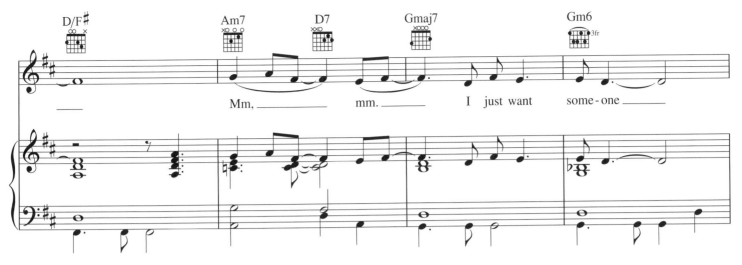

Mm, _____ mm. _____ I just want some-one _____

that I can talk ___ to. _____ I want you just ___ the way ___ you are. ___

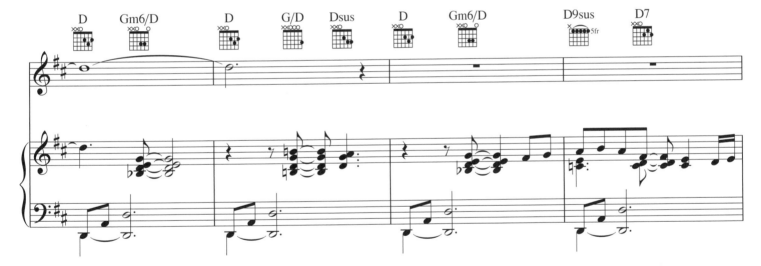

I need to know ___ that you ___ will al - ways be _____

the same old some-one that I _____ knew. Oh,

what will it take ___ till you ___ be-lieve _____ in me ___

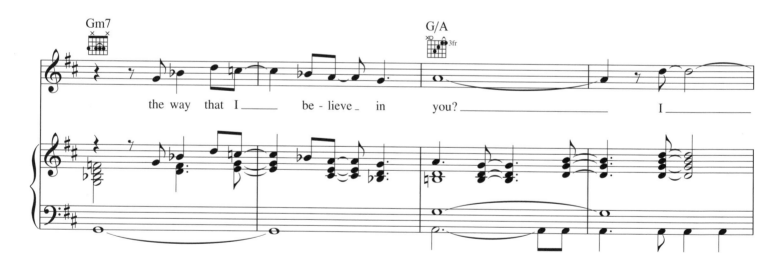

the way that I _____ be-lieve _ in you? _____ I _____

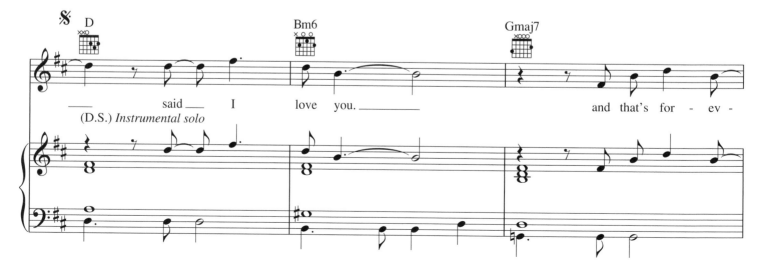

___ said ___ I love you. _____ and that's for - ev -

(D.S.) Instrumental solo

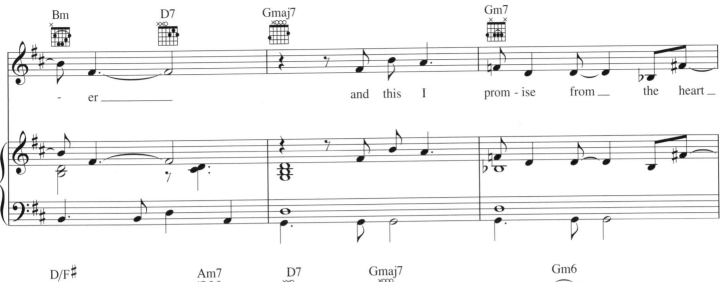

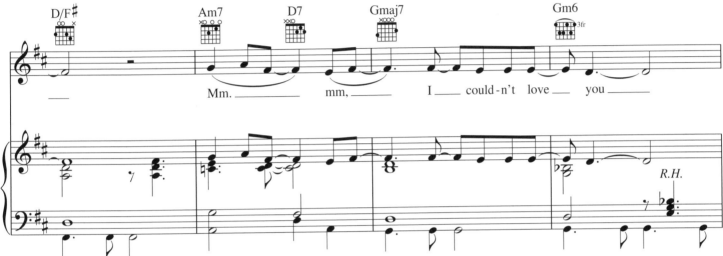

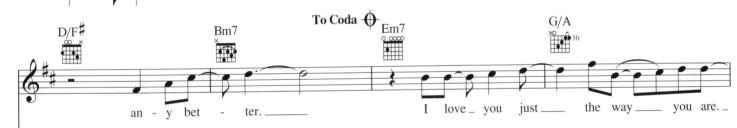

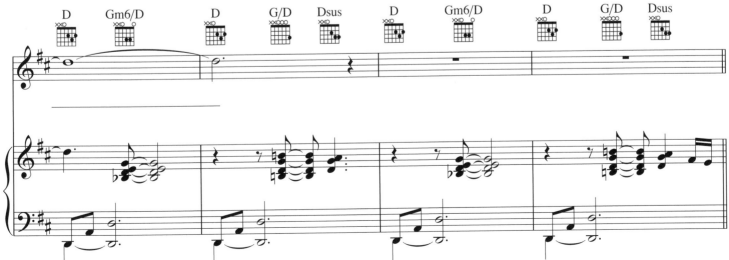

CODA

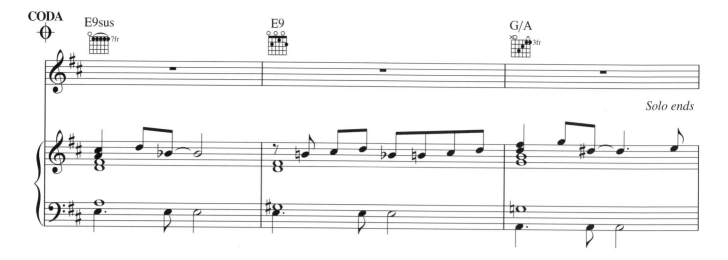

Solo ends

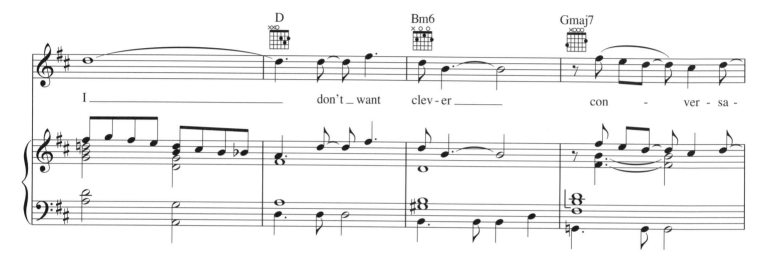

I _____ don't _ want clev - er _____ con - ver - sa-

-tion; I nev - er want _ to work _ that _ hard. _

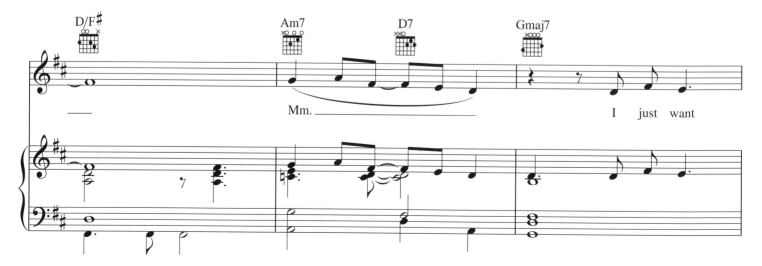

Mm. _____ I just want

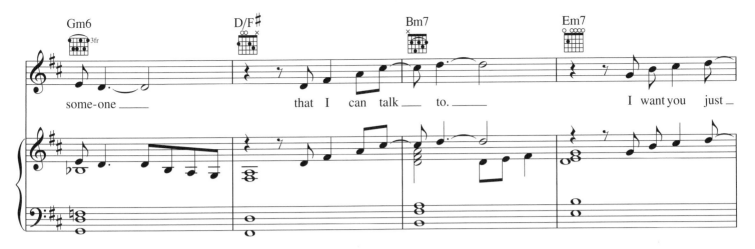

some-one ____ that I can talk ____ to. ____ I want you just ____

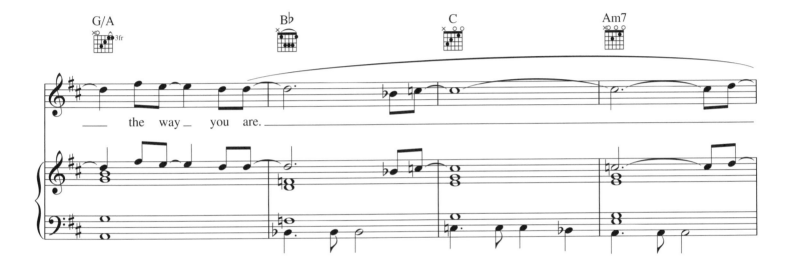

____ the way ____ you are. _____

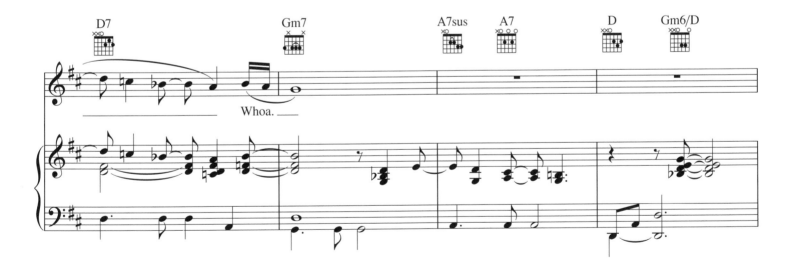

_____ Whoa. ____

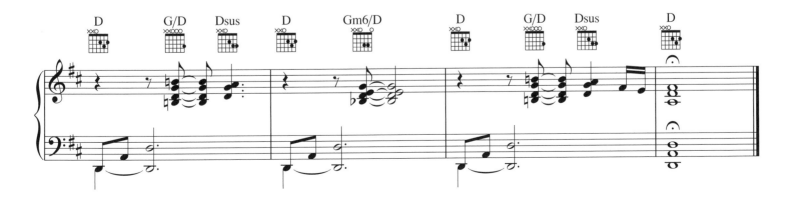

IT IS YOU
(I Have Loved)
from the DreamWorks Motion Picture SHREK

Words and Music by DANA GLOVER,
HARRY GREGSON-WILLIAMS, JOHN POWELL
and GAVIN GREENAWAY

What an un-ex-pect-ed way on this un-ex-pect-ed

day. __ Could it be this is where I ____ be - long?

It is you I ____ have loved all ____ a - long.

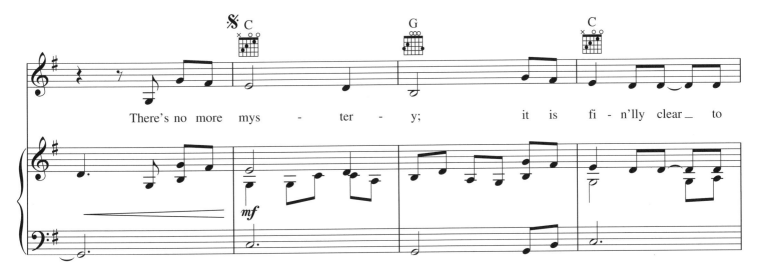

There's no more mys - ter - y; it is fi - n'lly clear __ to

me. You're the home my heart searched for so long.

And it is you I have loved all _____ a - long. _____

To Coda

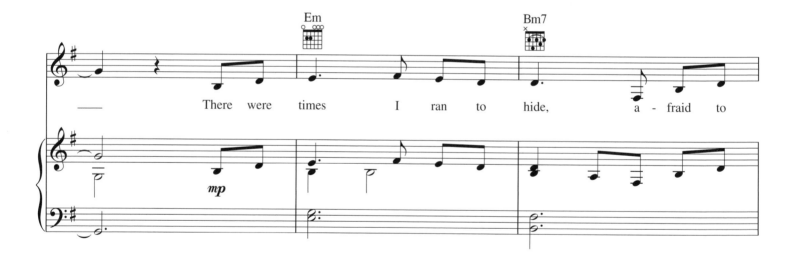

There were times I ran to hide, a - fraid to

show the oth - er side, a - lone in the night ___

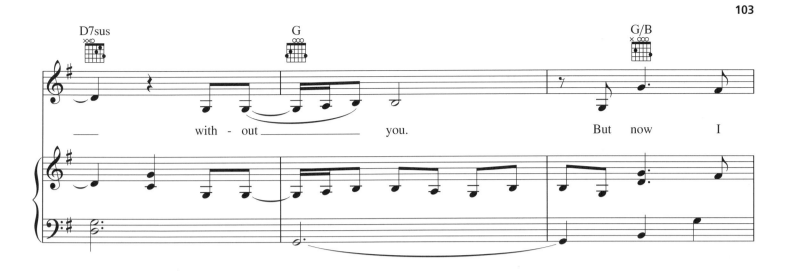

with - out _____ you. But now I

know just who you are, and I know you hold my

heart. Fi - nal - ly, this is where I be -

long. And it is you I _____ have

D.S. al Coda

loved all _____ a - long. _____ No more

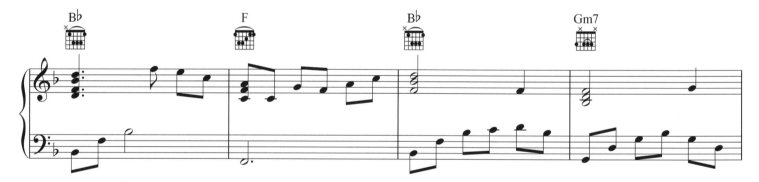

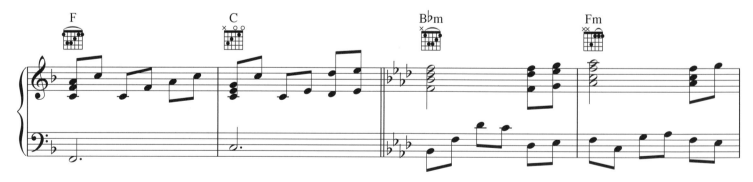

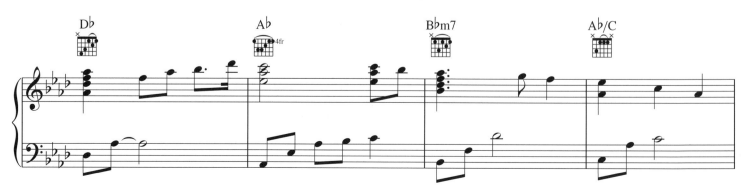

Oh, _____ o - ver _____ and

o - ver, I'm filled with ___ e - mo - tion.

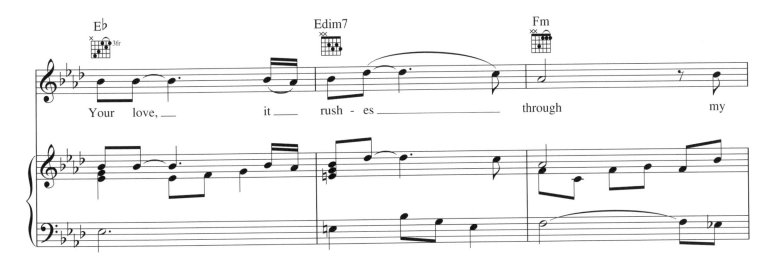

Your love, ___ it ___ rush - es _____ through my

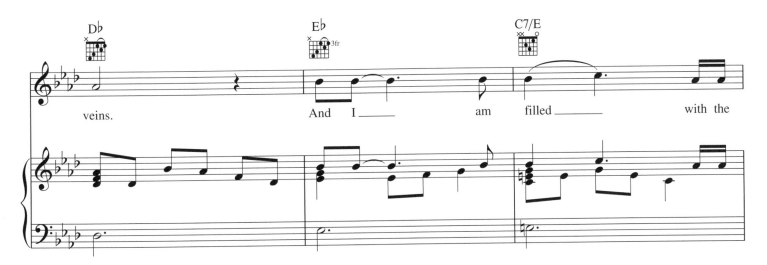

veins. And I _____ am filled _____ with the

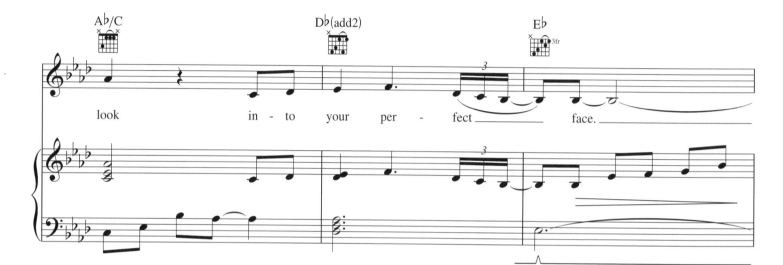

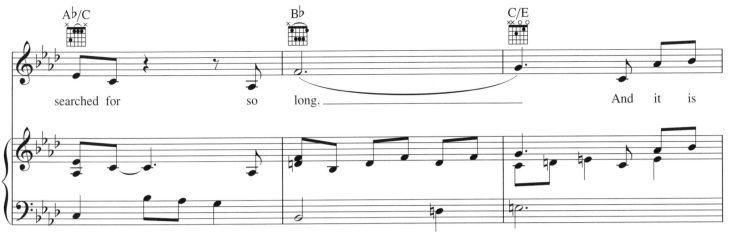

searched for so long. _____ And it is

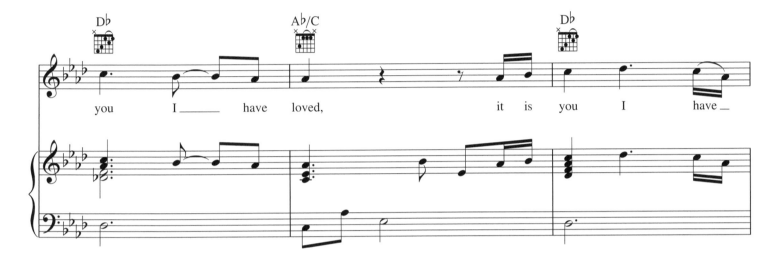

you I _____ have loved, it is you I have _____

Slowly, freely

loved, it is you I have loved all a-

long. _____

KEEP ME IN YOUR HEART

Words and Music by WARREN ZEVON
and JORGE CALDERON

keep me in ___ your heart for a - while. ___ When you

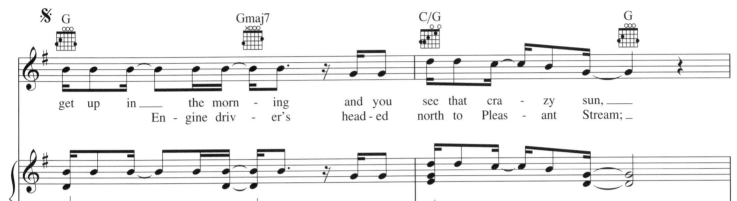

get up in ___ the morn - ing and you see that cra - zy sun, ___
En - gine driv - er's head - ed north to Pleas - ant Stream; ___

keep me in ___ your heart for a - while. ___ There's a
keep me in ___ your heart for a - while. ___ These

train leav - ing night - ly called _ "When all ___ is said and done;" _
wheels ___ keep turn - ing, but ___ they're run - ning out of steam; _

keep me in ____ your heart for a - while. ____
keep me in ____ your heart for a - while. ____

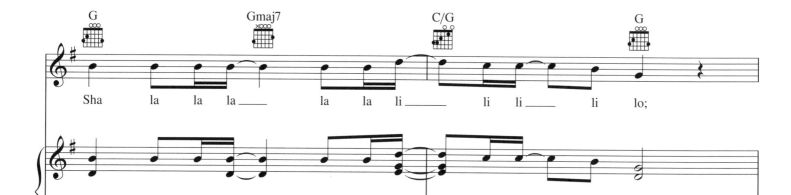

Sha la la la ____ la la li ____ li li ____ li lo;

keep me in ____ your heart ____ for a - while.

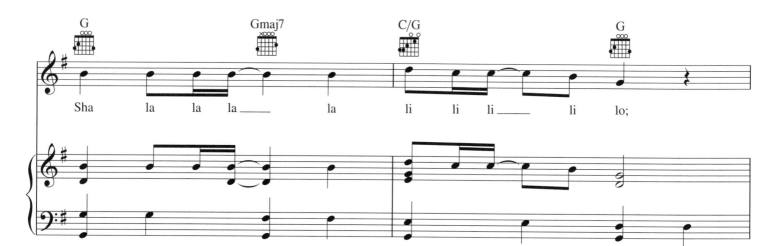

Sha la la la ____ la li li li ____ li lo;

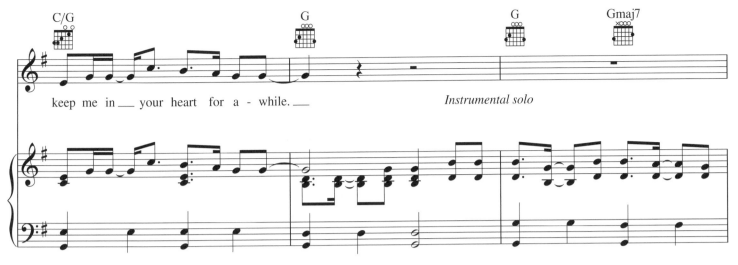

keep me in ___ your heart for a - while. ___   *Instrumental solo*

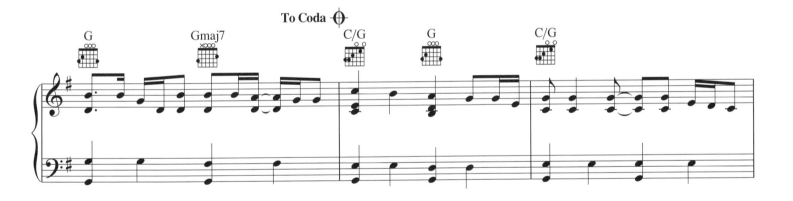

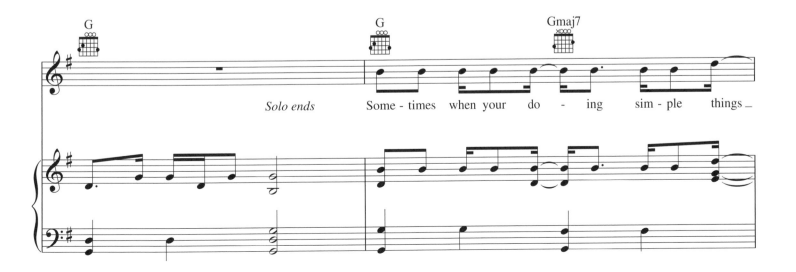

Solo ends   Some - times when your do - ing sim - ple things ___

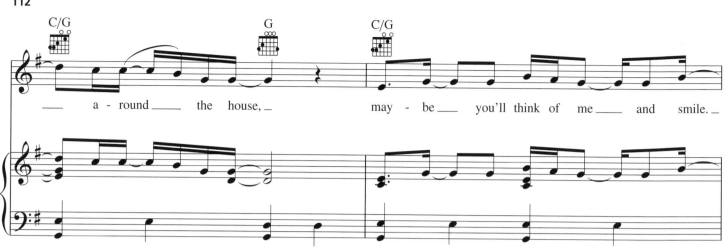

a - round _____ the house, _ may - be _ you'll think of me _ and smile. _

_____ You know I'm tied to you _ like the

but - tons on your blouse; _ keep me in _ your heart for a - while.

_____ Hold me in _ your thoughts, _

take me to ___ your dreams, ___ touch me as ___ I fall ___ in - to view. ___

___ And when the win - ter comes, ___

D.S. al Coda

keep the fi - res lit, ___ and I will be right ___ next to you.

CODA

Solo ends Keep me in ___ your heart for a - while. ___

rit.

LONGER

Words and Music by
DAN FOGELBERG

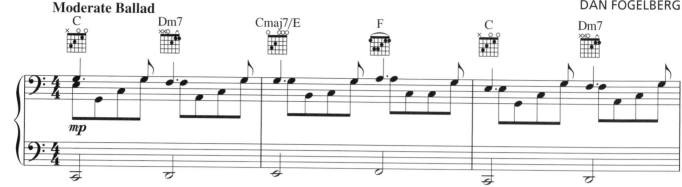

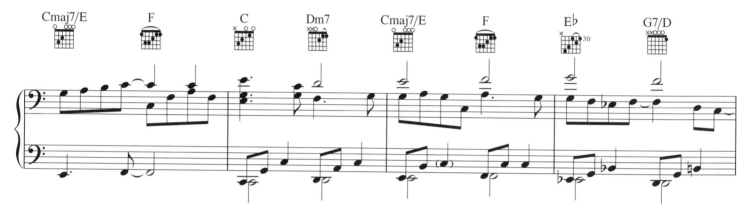

Long - er than ___ there've been fish - es in the o - cean,
Strong - er than ___ an - y moun - tain ca - the - dral,
Through the years ___ as the fi - re starts to mel - low,

high - er than ___ an - y bird ev - er flew, ___
tru - er than ___ an - y tree ev - er grew, ___
burn - ing lines ___ in the book of our lives,

long - er than ___ there've been
deep - er than ___ an - y
though the bind - ing cracks ___ and the pag-

CODA

I'll be in love __ with you. __

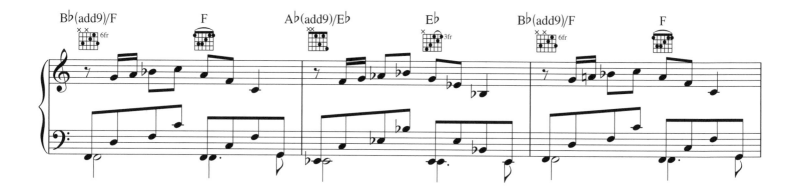

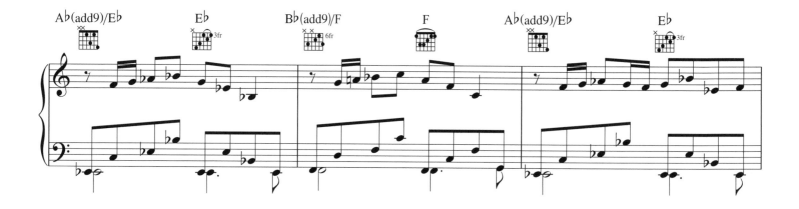

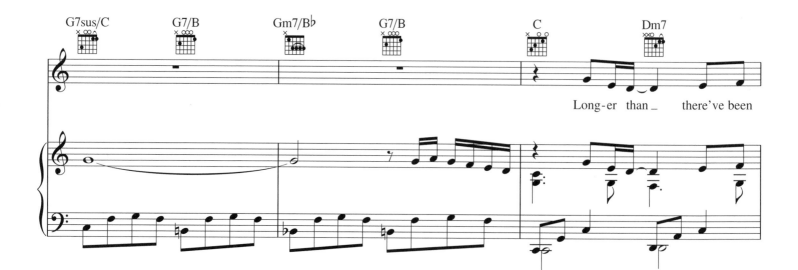

Long-er than __ there've been

fish - es __ in the o - cean, __ high - er than __ an - y bird ev - er flew, _

long - er than __ there've been stars up in the heav - ens, ____

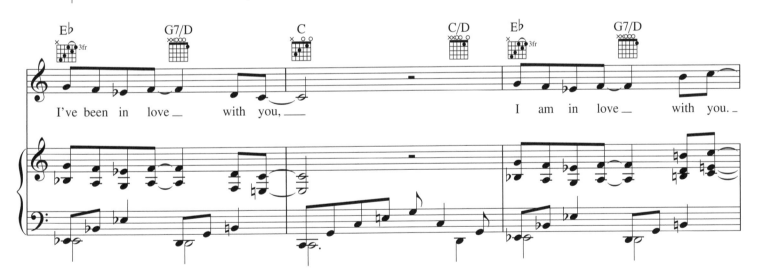

I've been in love __ with you, __ I am in love __ with you. _

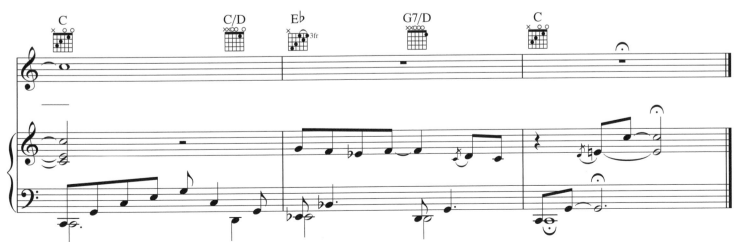

MAKE YOU FEEL MY LOVE

Words and Music by
BOB DYLAN

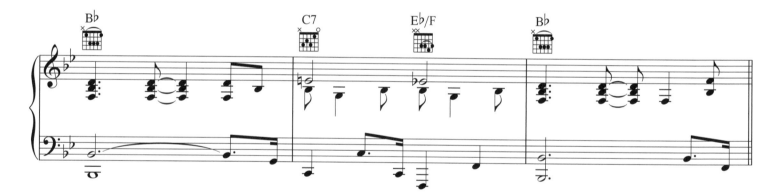

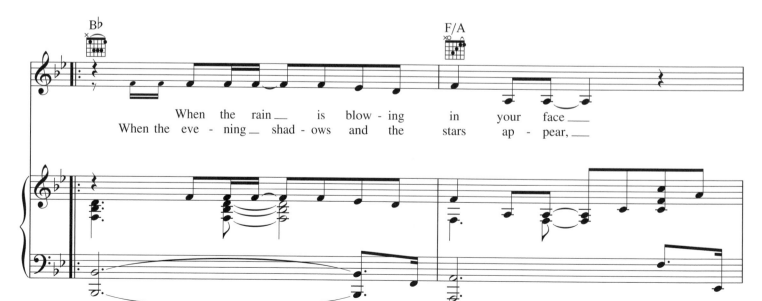

When the rain __ is blow-ing in your face __
When the eve-ning __ shad-ows and the stars ap-pear, __

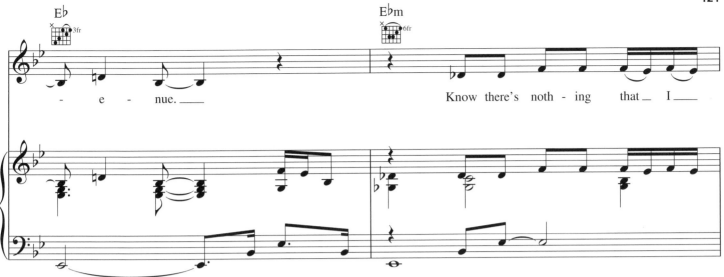

-e -nue. ___ Know there's noth - ing that __ I ___

would - n't do ___ to make you feel my love. ___

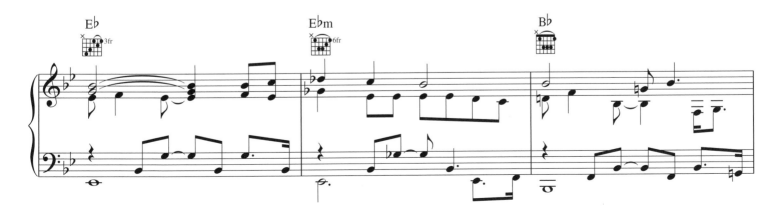

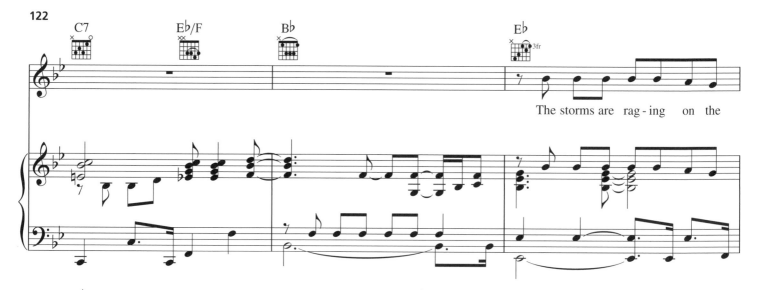

The storms are rag-ing on the

roll - ing sea ___ and on the high - way of re - gret. ___

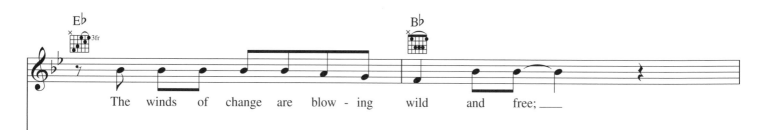

The winds of change are blow-ing wild and free; ___

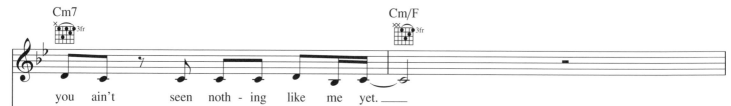

you ain't seen noth-ing like me yet. ___

MORE THAN WORDS

Words and Music by NUNO BETTENCOURT
and GARY CHERONE

Moderately slow

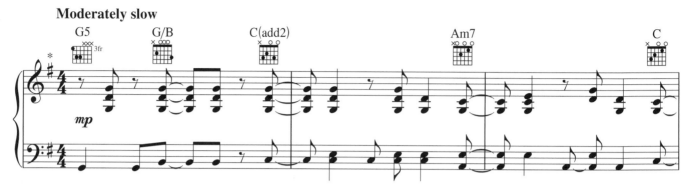

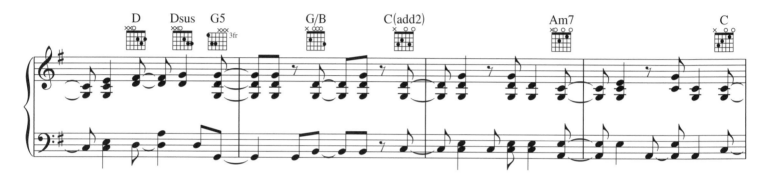

Say - in' "I ___ love ___ you" is
Now that I've ___ tried ___ to

not the words ___ I want ___ to ___ hear ___ from you. ___ It's not that I ___
talk to you ___ and make ___ you ___ un - der - stand, ___ all ___ you ___

* Recorded a half step lower.

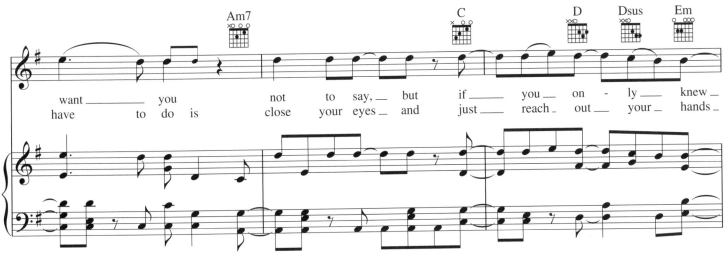

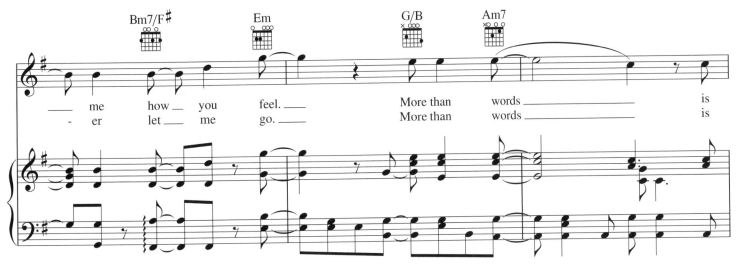

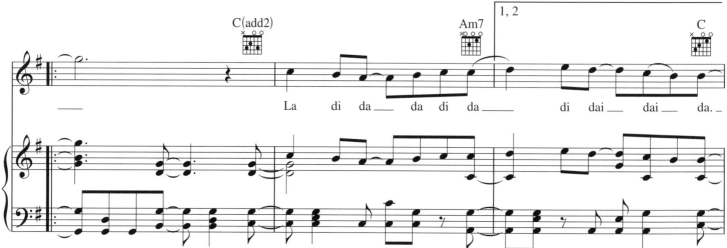

MUSIC OF MY HEART

Words and Music by
DIANE WARREN

You'll nev-er know _____ what you've done for me, _____ what your
You were the one _____ al-ways on my side, _____ al-ways

faith in me ___ has done for my ___ soul. _____
stand-ing by, ___ see-ing me ___ through. _____

You'll nev-er know the gift ___ you've ___ giv-en me; _____ I'll car-ry
You were the song ___ that al - ways _____ made me sing; _____ I'm sing-ing this

Recorded a half step higher in B major.

it with me. _____

for you. _____

_____ of days _____ be - fore, when you made me _____ hope for some - thing bet - ter and made me

_____ of where _____ I've been _____ and of the _____ one who knew _____ me bet - ter than an - y - one

_____ reach for some - thing more. _ } You taught me to run, _____ you taught me to fly, _____ helped me to free _____

ev - er will _____ a - gain. _

_____ the me _____ in - side, _____ helped me hear the mu - sic of _____ my heart, helped me hear the

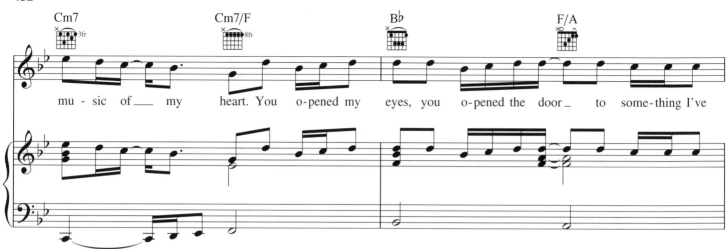

mu - sic of ___ my heart. You o-pened my eyes, you o-pened the door ___ to some-thing I've

nev - er known ___ be-fore, and your love is the mu - sic of ___ my heart.

love is the mu - sic of ___ my heart. What you taught ___ me, on - ly

your love could ev - er teach ___ me. You got through where no one could reach ___ me be - fore. ___ (Be -

you taught me to fly, __ helped me to free __ the me __ in - side, __ helped me hear the

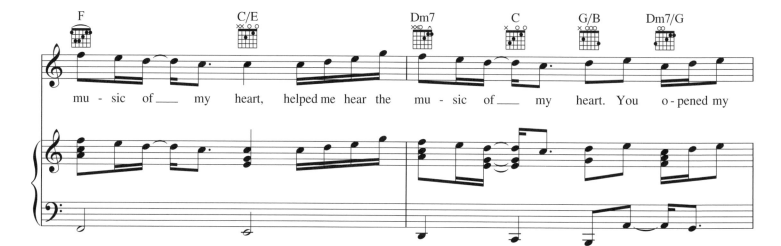

mu - sic of __ my heart, helped me hear the mu - sic of __ my heart. You o - pened my

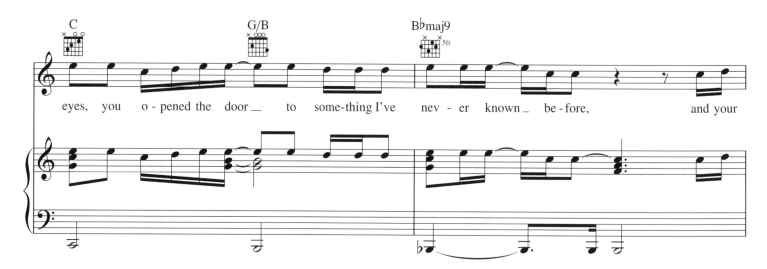

eyes, you o - pened the door __ to some-thing I've nev - er known __ be - fore, __ and your

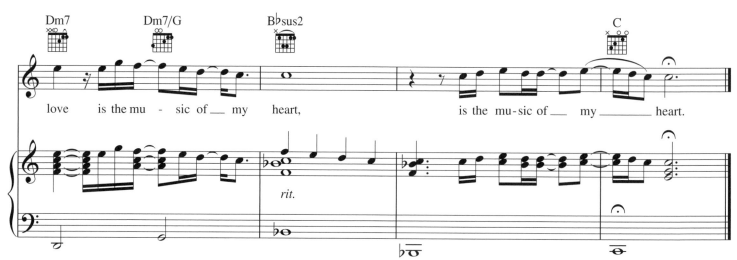

love is the mu - sic of __ my heart, is the mu - sic of __ my __ heart.

rit.

STRAIGHT FROM THE HEART

Words and Music by BRYAN ADAMS
and ERIC KAGNA

Moderate Rock Ballad

I could start dream-ing but it nev-er ends.___ As long as you're gone___ we may as well___ pre-tend. I've been dream-ing___ straight from the heart.___

make {an-oth-er / one more} start. ___ You know I'll nev-er go ___ as long as I know ___

1

___ it's com-in' straight from the heart. ___

2

___ it's com-in' straight from the heart. _

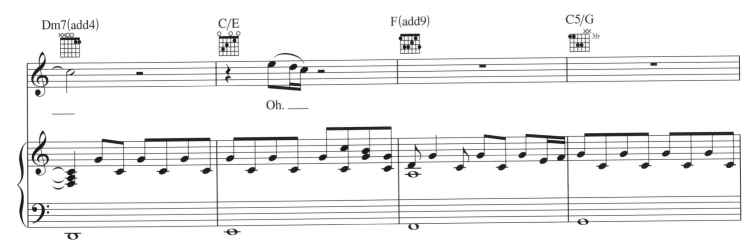

Oh. ___

Don't ev-er leave ___ me, dar - lin'.

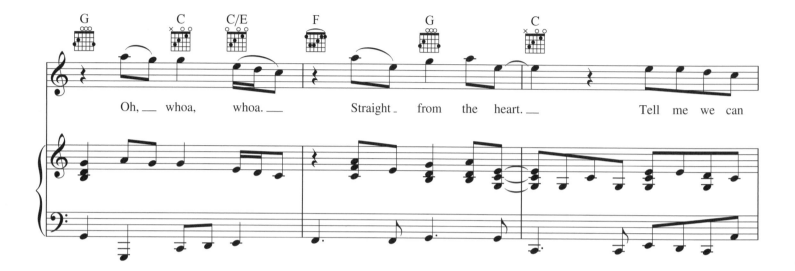

Oh, __ whoa, whoa. __ Straight __ from the heart. __ Tell me we can

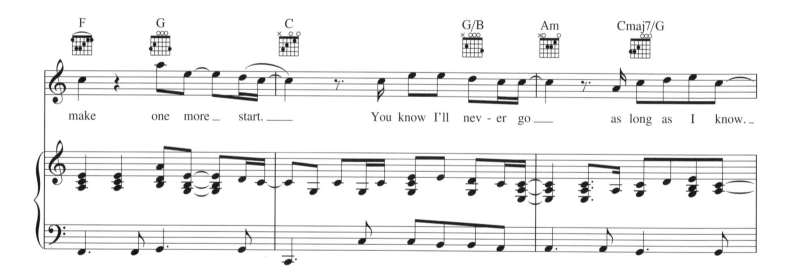

make one more __ start. __ You know I'll nev - er go __ as long as I know. __

__ Give it to me now, __ straight __ from the heart. __ Tell me we can

MY HEART WILL GO ON
(Love Theme from 'Titanic')
from the Paramount and Twentieth Century Fox Motion Picture TITANIC

Music by JAMES HORNER
Lyric by WILL JENNINGS

Moderately

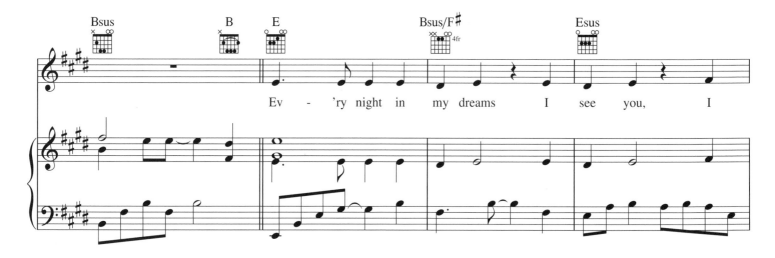

Ev - 'ry night in my dreams I see you, I

feel you, that is how I know you go on.

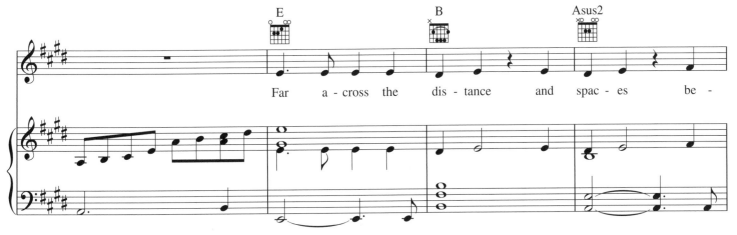

Far a-cross the dis-tance and spac-es be-

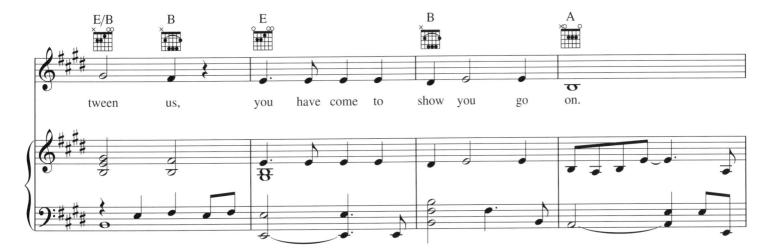

tween us, you have come to show you go on.

Near, far, wher-ev-er you are,

I be-lieve that the heart does go on.

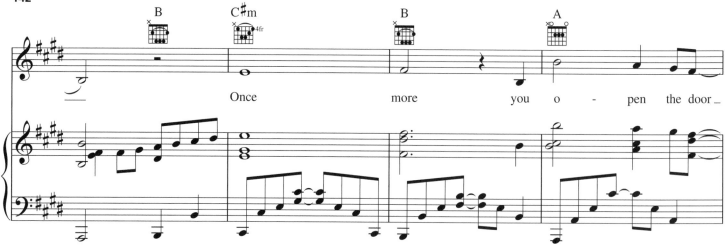

Once more you o - pen the door _

_ and you're here in my heart, and my heart will go

To Coda ⊕

on and on.

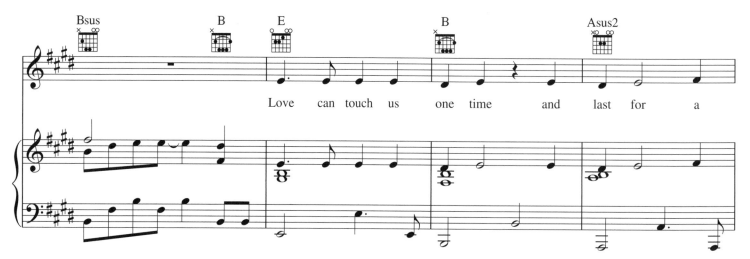

Love can touch us one time and last for a

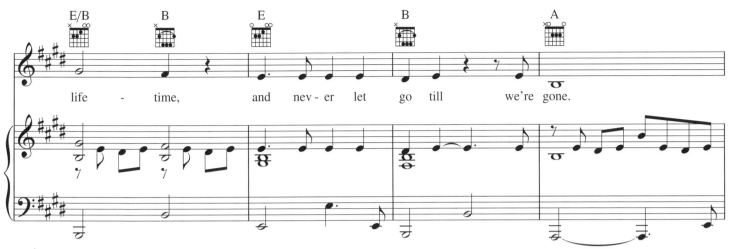

life - time, and nev-er let go till we're gone.

Love was when I loved you; one true time I

hold to. In my life we'll al - ways go on.

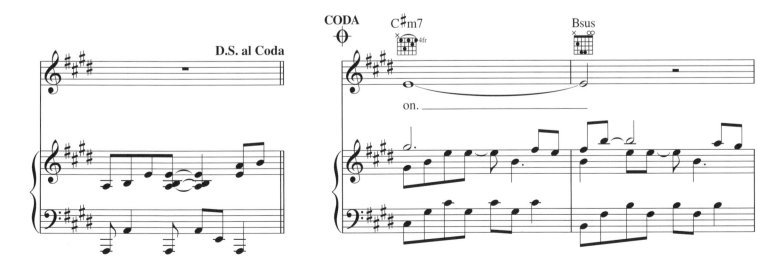

D.S. al Coda

CODA

on. _____

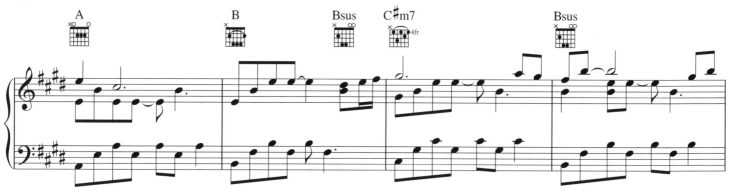

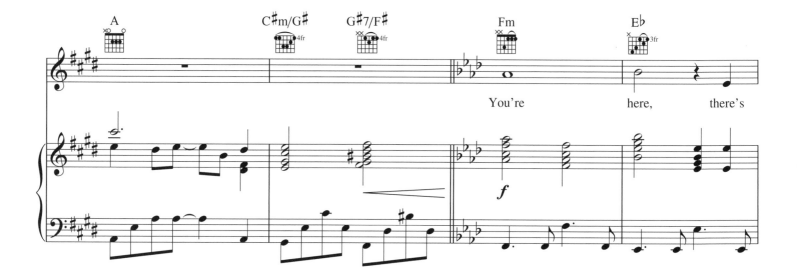

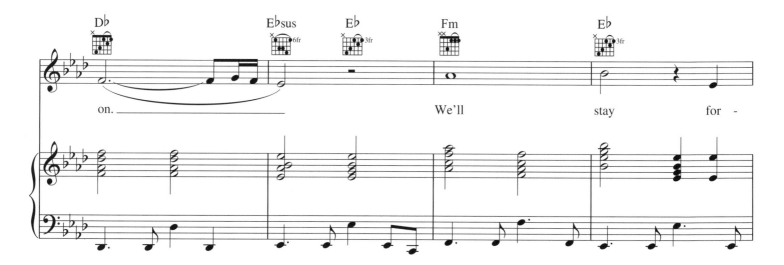

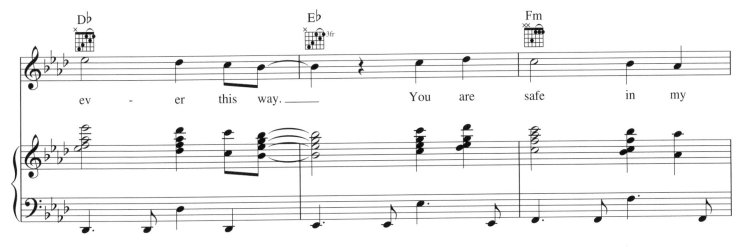

ev - er this way. ___ You are safe in my

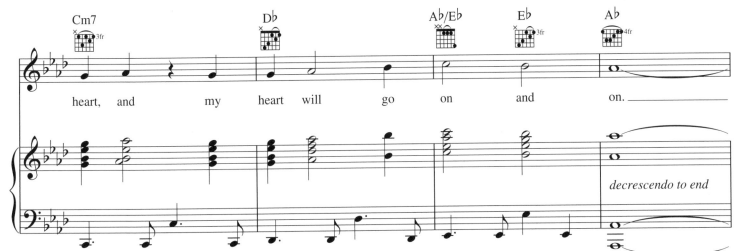

heart, and my heart will go on and on. ___

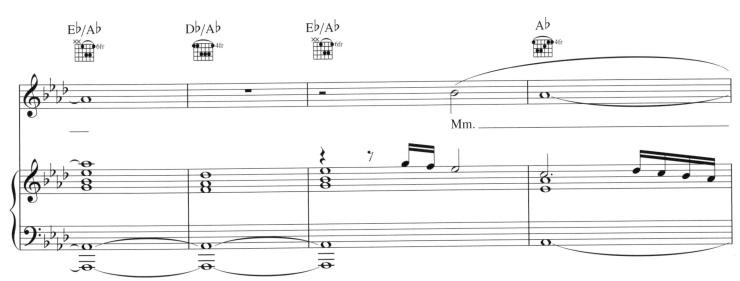

Mm. ___

decrescendo to end

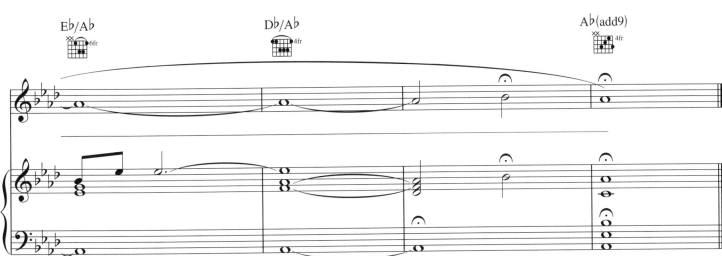

NOW AND FOREVER

Words and Music by
RICHARD MARX

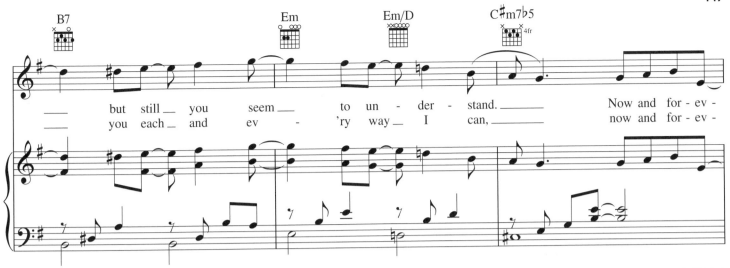

but still __ you seem __ to un - der - stand. _____ Now and for - ev -
you each __ and ev - 'ry way __ I can, _____ now and for - ev -

- er, _____ I will be __ your man. _____
- er, _____ I will be __ your man. _

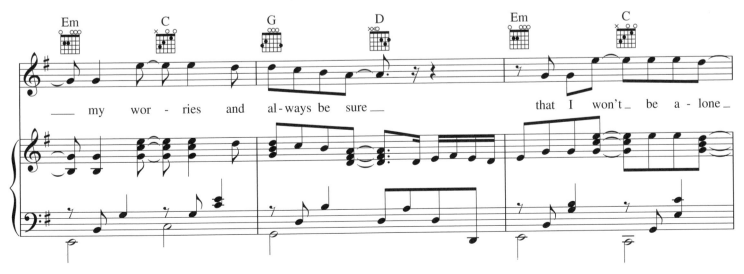

_____ Now I can rest __

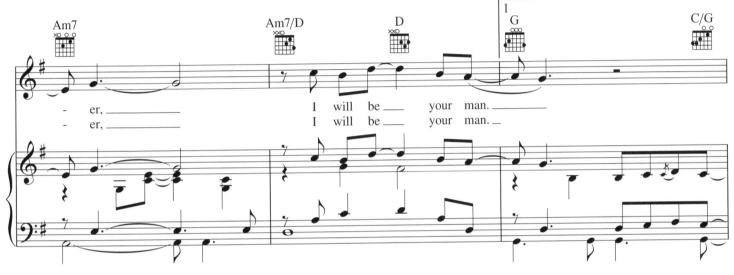

__ my wor - ries and al - ways be sure __ that I won't __ be a - lone __

-n't touch the sand, _____ now and for - ev - er, _____

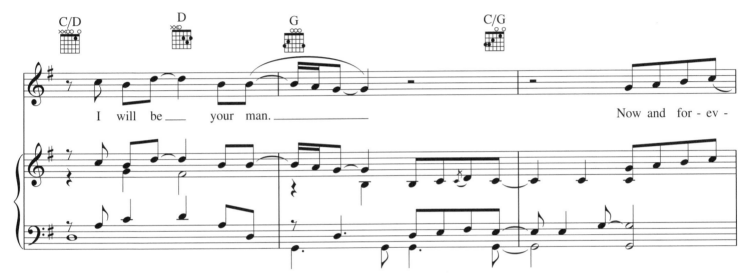

I will be _____ your man. _____ Now and for - ev -

- er, I will be _____ your

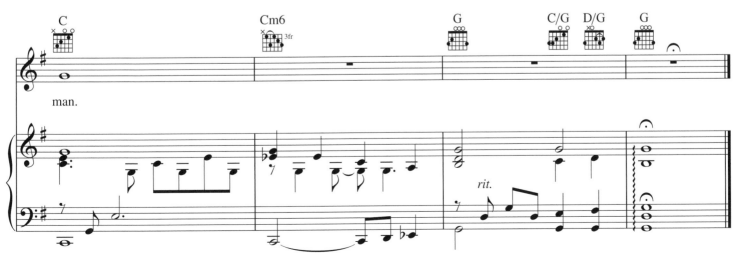

man.

rit.

OPEN ARMS

Words and Music by STEVE PERRY
and JONATHAN CAIN

Moderately slow

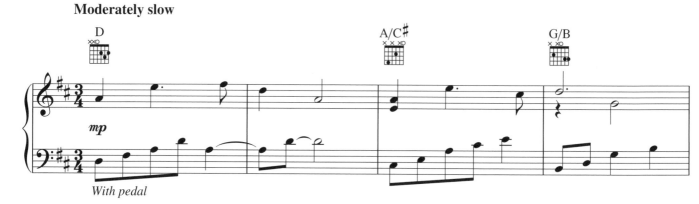

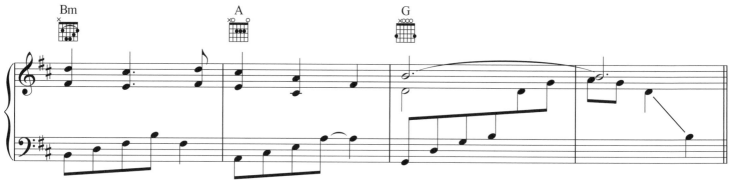

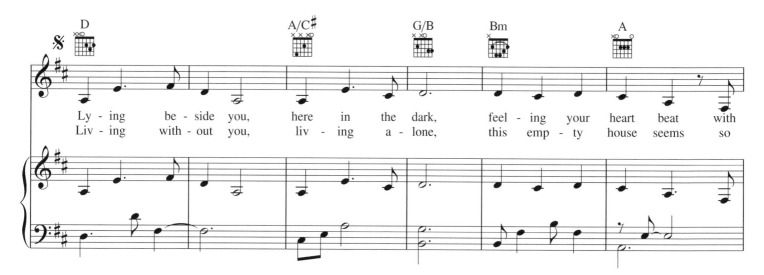

Ly - ing be - side you, here in the dark, feel - ing your heart beat with
Liv - ing with - out you, liv - ing a - lone, this emp - ty house seems so

mine. Soft - ly you whis - per; you're so sin -
cold. Want - ing to hold you, want - ing you

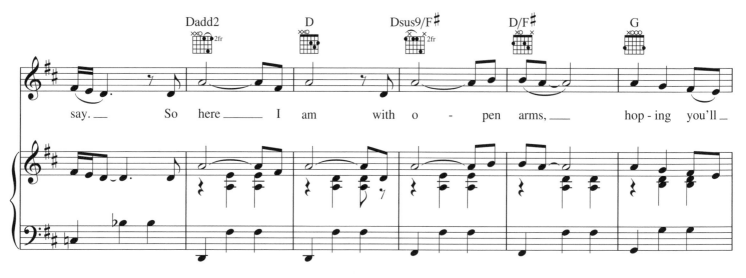

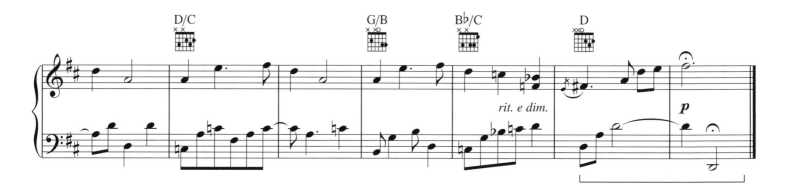

TEARS IN HEAVEN

featured in the Motion Picture RUSH

Words and Music by ERIC CLAPTON
and WILL JENNINGS

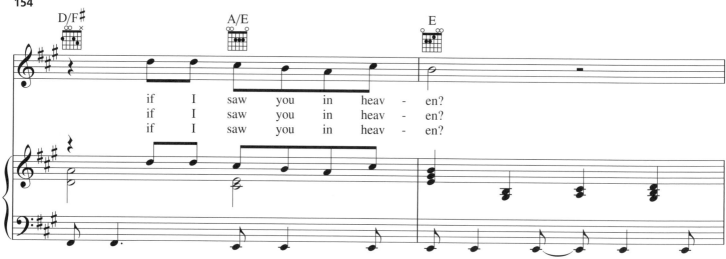

if I saw you in heav - en?
if I I saw you in heav - en?
if I I saw you in heav - en?

(1., 3.) I must be strong ___ and car - ry on ___
(2.) I'll find my way ___ through night and day ___

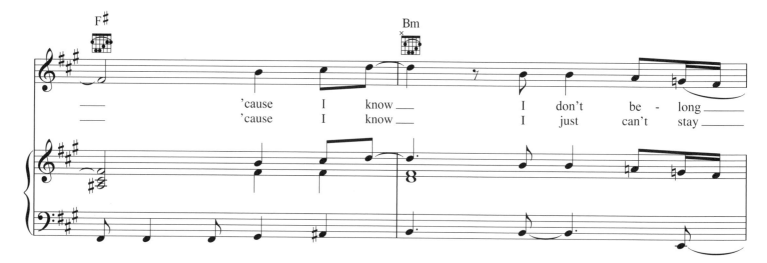

___ 'cause I know ___ I don't be - long ___
___ 'cause I know ___ I just can't stay ___

To Coda

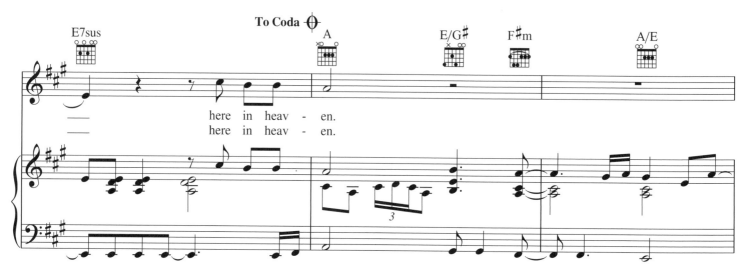

___ here in heav - en.
___ here in heav - en.

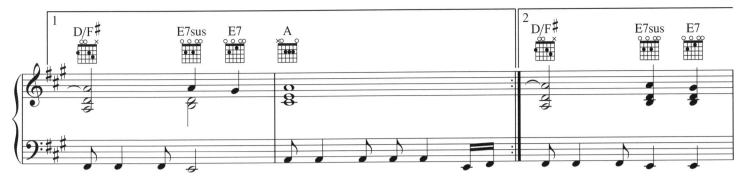

Time can bring you down, _____

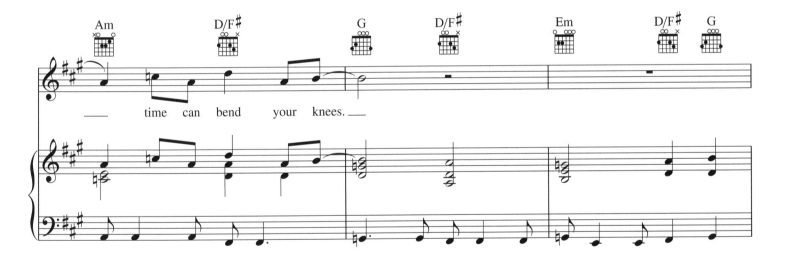

_____ time can bend your knees. _____

Time can break the heart, _____ have you beg - gin' please, _____ beg - gin' please. _

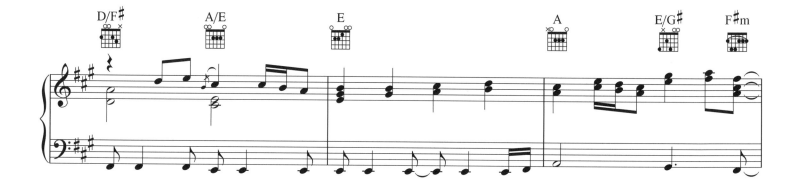

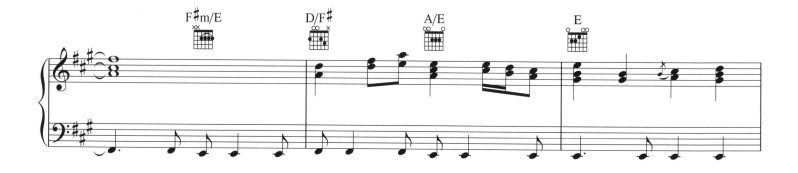

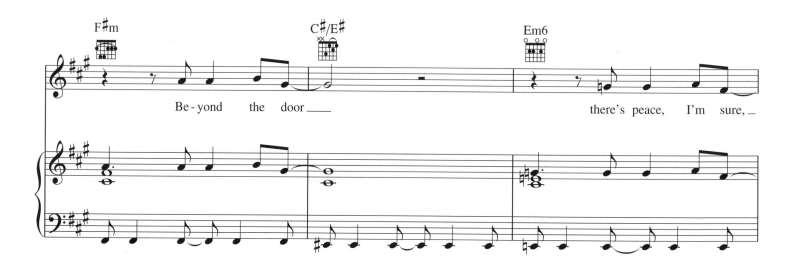

Be - yond the door ___ there's peace, I'm sure, ___

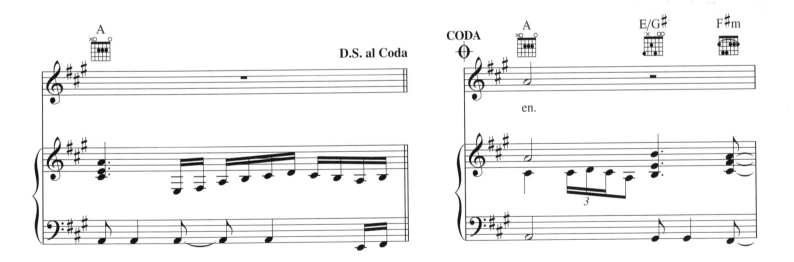

RIGHT HERE WAITING

Words and Music by
RICHARD MARX

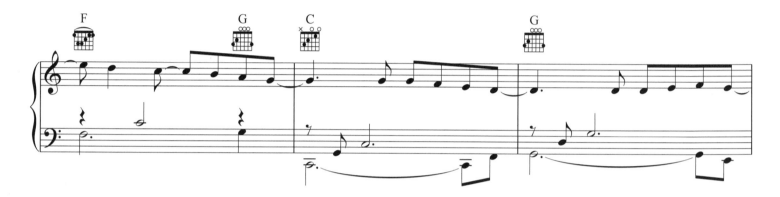

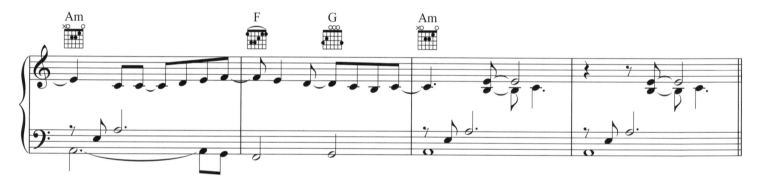

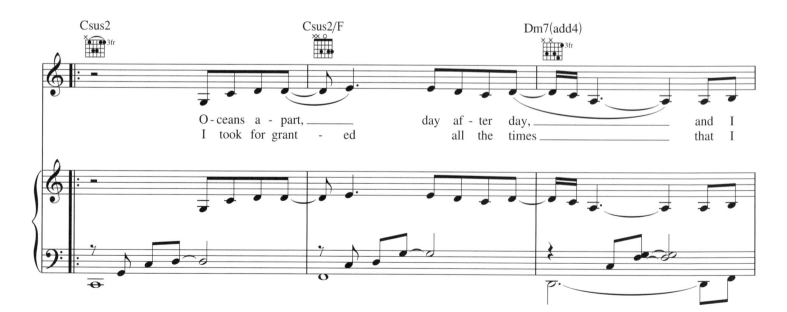

O-ceans a-part,_____ day af-ter day,_____ and I

I took for grant - ed all the times _____ that I

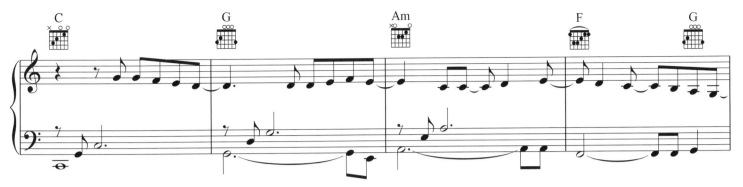

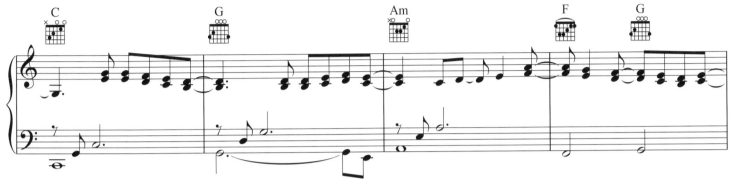

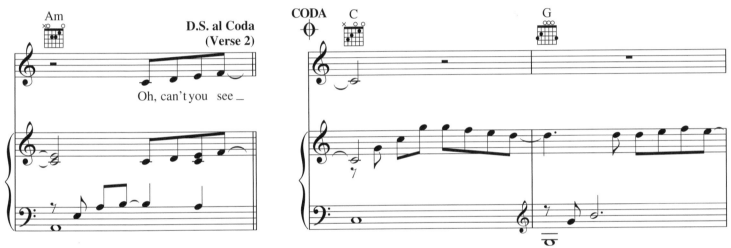

Oh, can't you see

Wait - ing for you.

WILL YOU STILL LOVE ME

Words and Music by DAVID FOSTER,
RICHARD BASKIN and TOM KEANE

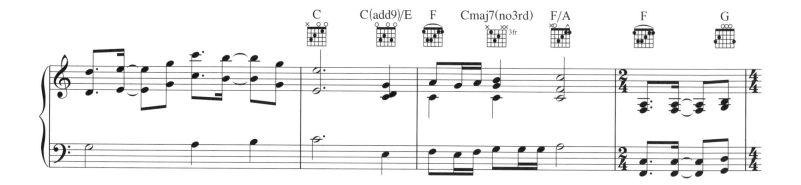

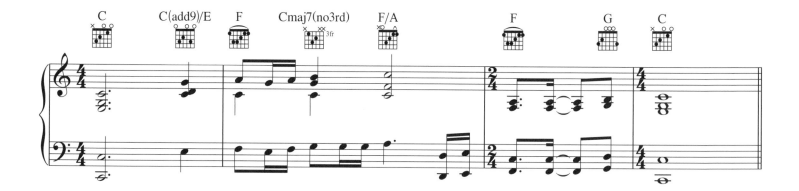

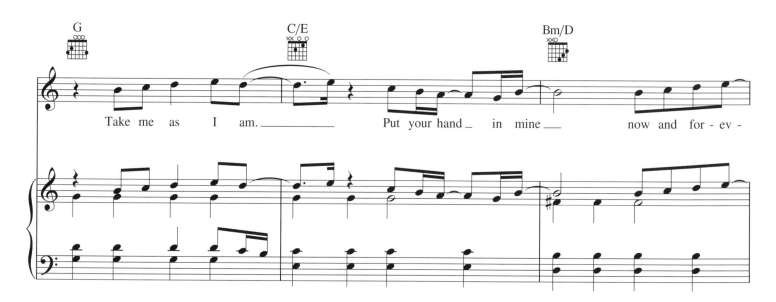

Take me as I am. _____ Put your hand _ in mine _ now and for- ev-

Ev-'ry road leads to your door,__ ev-'ry step I take for-ev-er-more. Just say you love me for the__

rest of your life. I got a lot of love and I don't wan na let go.____

Will you still love me for the__ rest of my life? ____'Cause I can't go on, no, I can't go

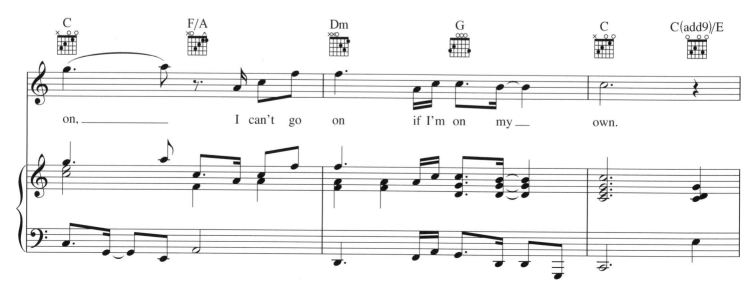

on, _____ I can't go on if I'm on my__ own.

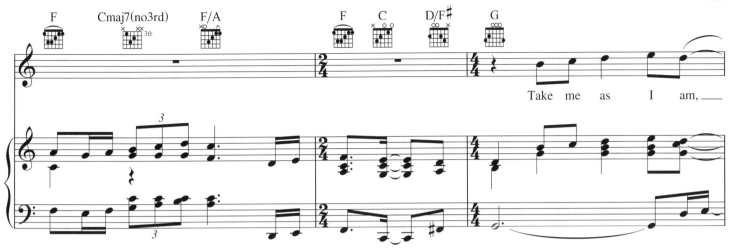

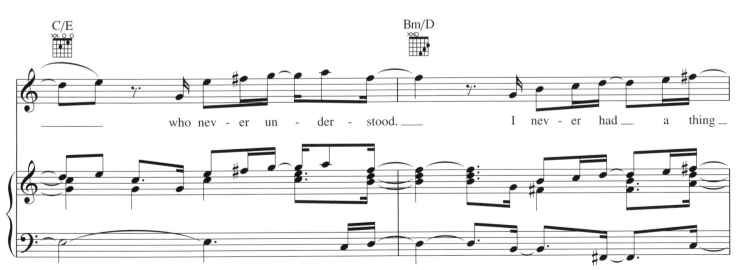

to prove. Till there was you, you, and me, then it

all came clear so sud-den-ly. How close to you, that I wan-na be.

Just say you love me for the rest of your life. I

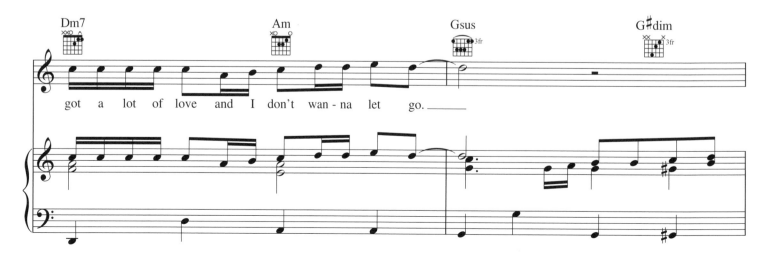

got a lot of love and I don't wan-na let go.

Will you still love me for the ___ rest of my life? 'Cause I can't go

on, no, I can't go on, _____ I can't go

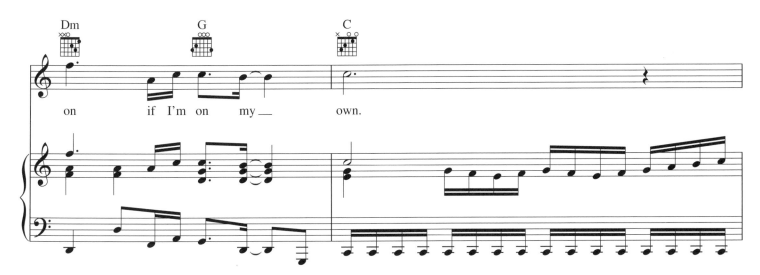

on if I'm on my ___ own.

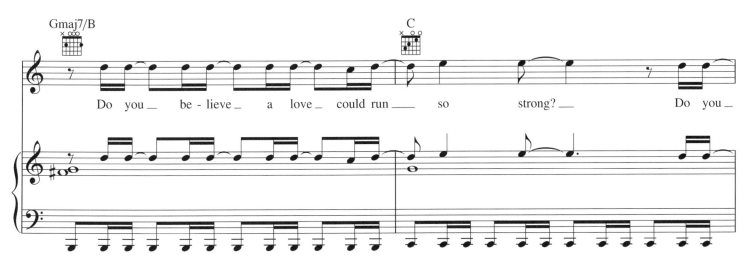

Do you ___ be-lieve ___ a love ___ could run ___ so strong? ___ Do you ___

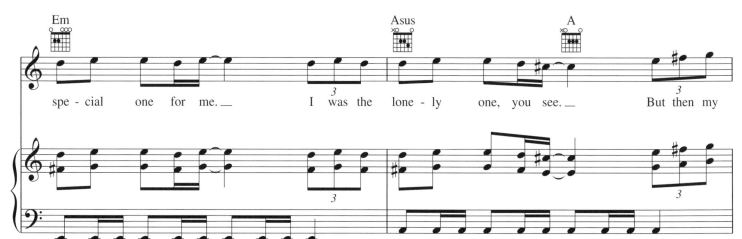

got a lot of love and I don't wan-na let go. _____

Will you still love me for the ___ rest of my life? ___ 'Cause I can't go

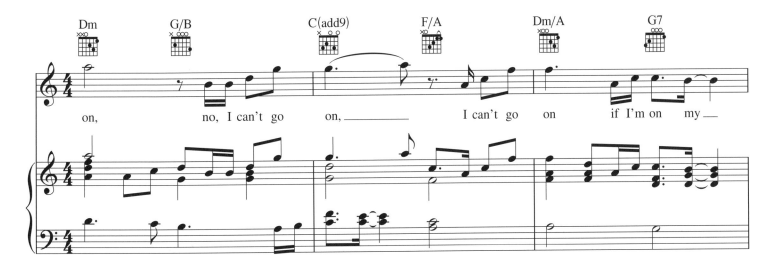

on, no, I can't go on, _____ I can't go on if I'm on my ___

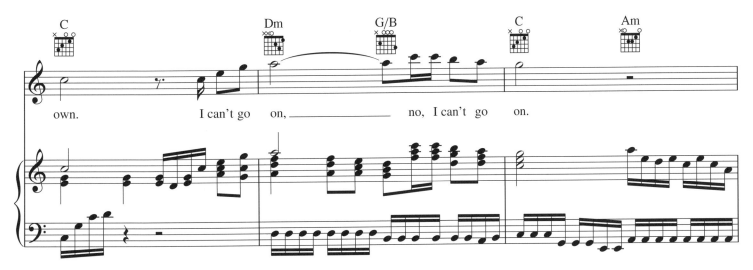

own. I can't go on, _____ no, I can't go on.

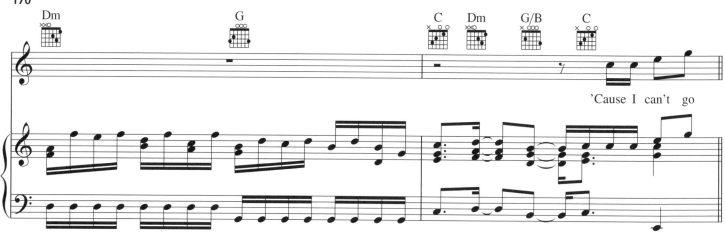

'Cause I can't go

on, _____ no, I can't go on, _____ I can't go
(Will you _ still love _ me?) (Just say _ you love _ me.)

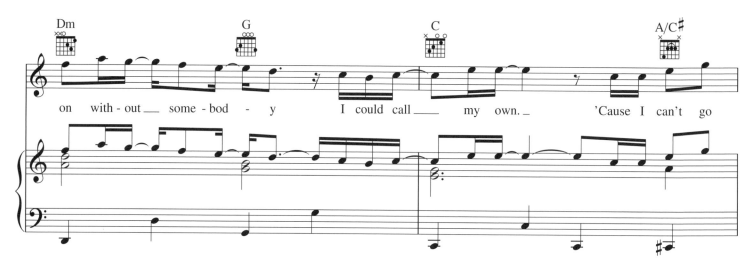

on with-out _ some-bod - y I could call _ my own. _ 'Cause I can't go

on, _____ no, I can't go on. Just stay a -
(Will you _ still love _ me?) (Just say _ you love _ me.)

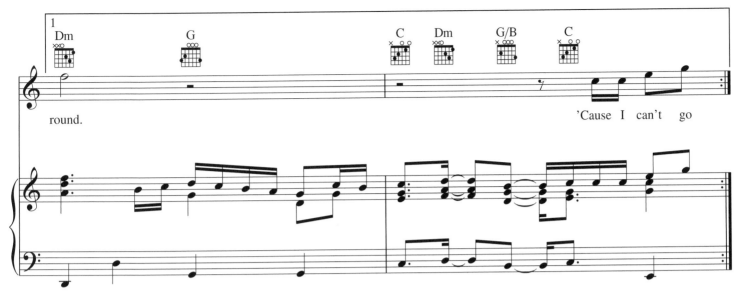

round.   'Cause I can't go

round   and nev-er be ___ a - lone. ___

With pedal

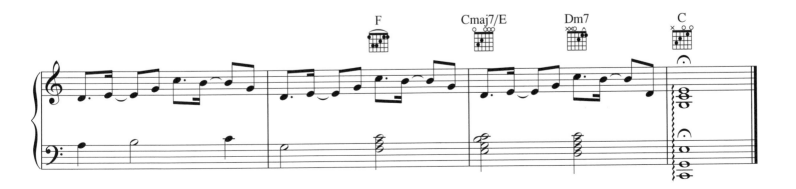

THE WIND BENEATH MY WINGS

from the Original Motion Picture BEACHES

Words and Music by LARRY HENLEY
and JEFF SILBAR

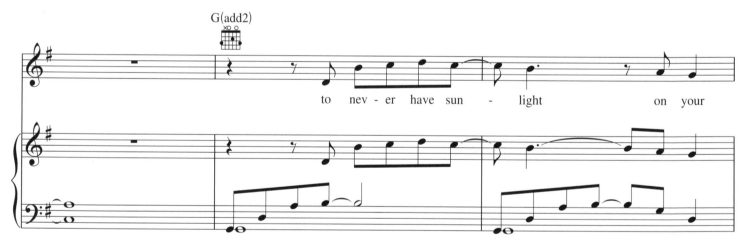

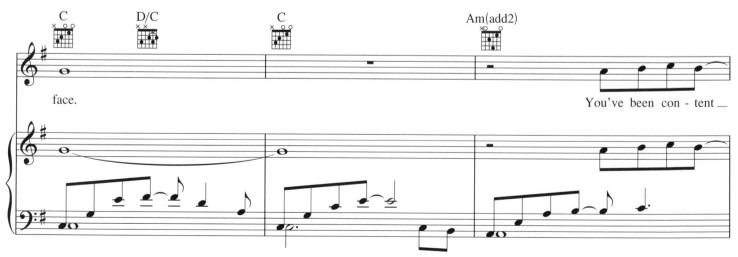

to let me shine,

you al-ways walked __ the step be-hind. __

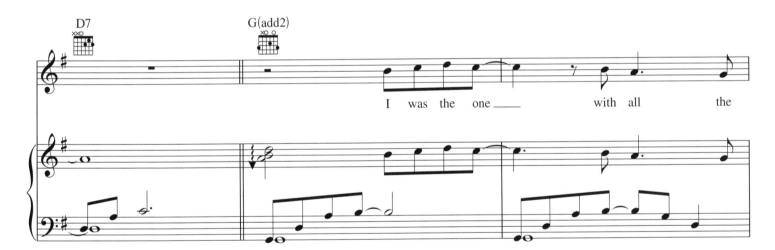

I was the one __ with all the

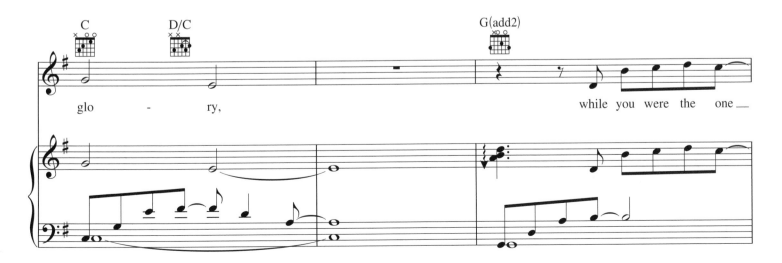

glo - ry, while you were the one __

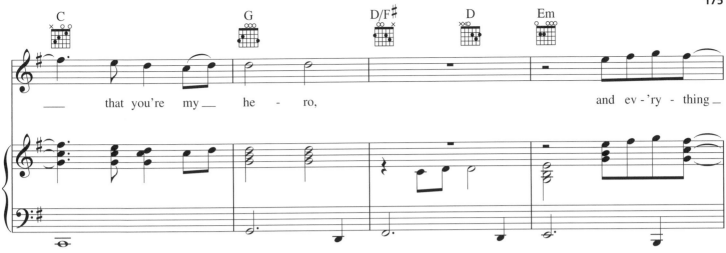

that you're my ___ he - ro, and ev -'ry - thing ___

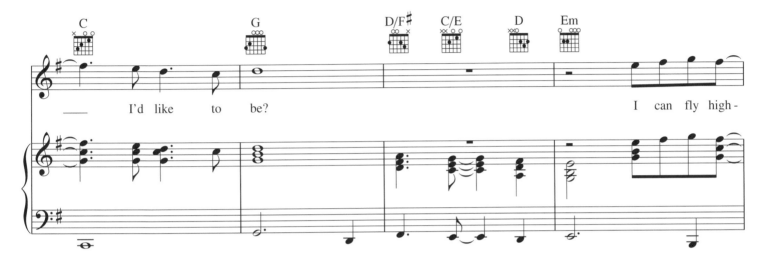

___ I'd like to be? I can fly high -

- er than an ea - gle, _____ 'cause you are the wind ___

To Coda ⊕

___ be - neath my wings.

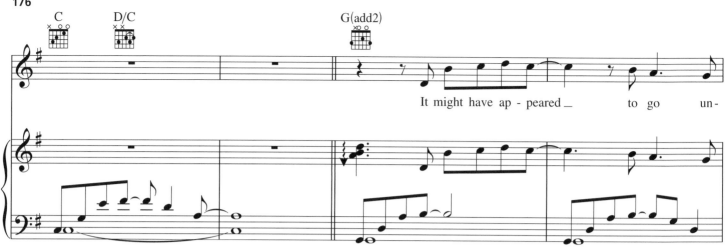

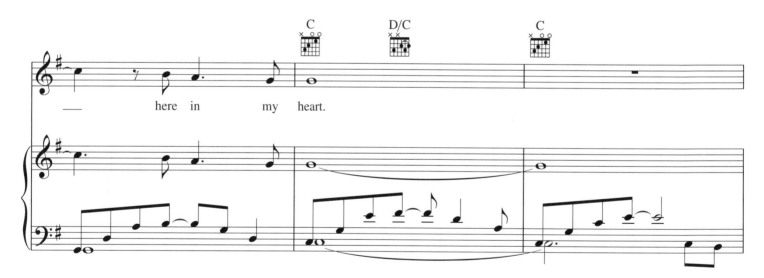

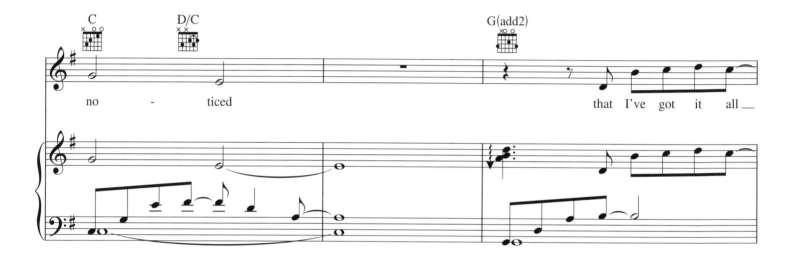

I would be noth - in' with - out

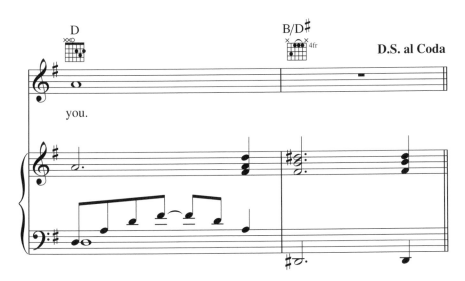

you.

D.S. al Coda

CODA

wings.

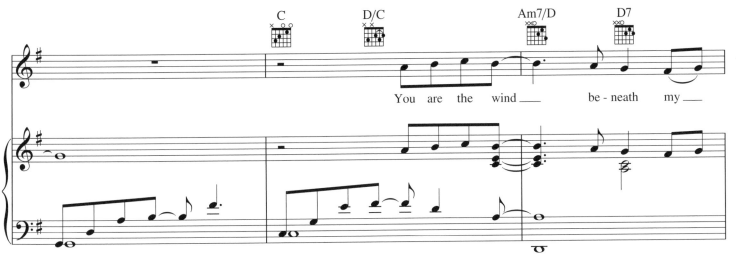

You are the wind ___ be - neath my ___

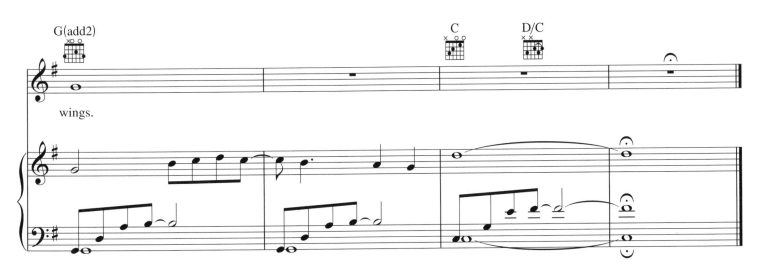

wings.

YOU ARE LOVED
(Don't Give Up)

Words and Music by
THOMAS SALTER

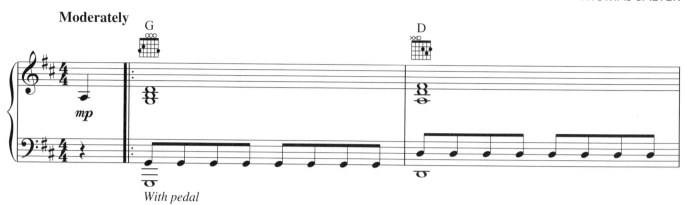

With pedal

Don't give up; _____ it's just the
Don't give up; _____ it's just the

weight _____ of the world. _____ When
hurt _____ that you hide. _____ When

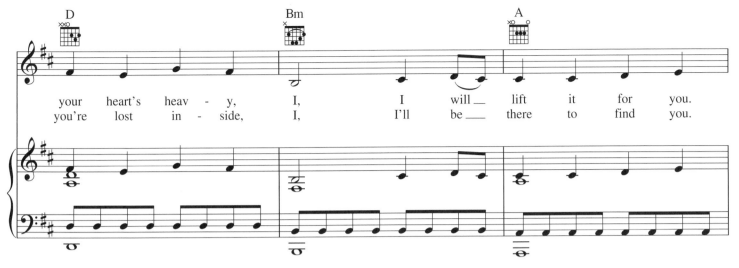

your heart's heav - y,   I,   I will __ lift it for you.
you're lost in - side,   I,   I'll be __ there to find you.

Don't give up __
Don't give up __

be - cause you want __   to be heard. __
be - cause you want __   to burn bright. __

__ If si - lence keeps you,   I,   I will __
__ If dark - ness blinds you,   I,   I will __

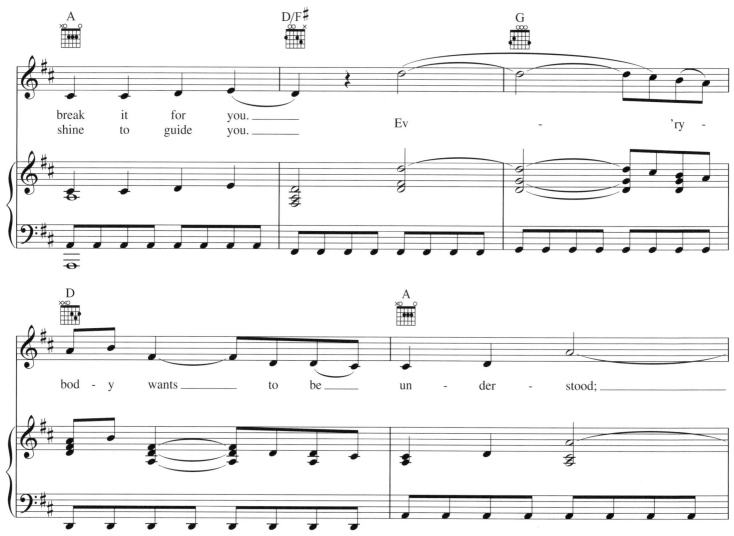

break it for you. _____
shine to for guide you. _____ Ev - - 'ry -

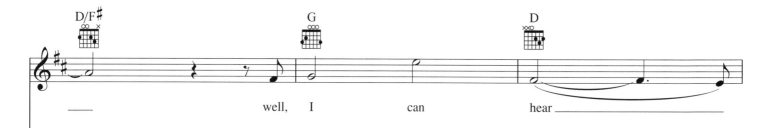

bod - y wants _____ to be _____ un - der - stood; _____

_____ well, I can hear _____

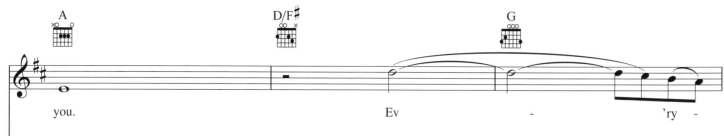

you. Ev - - 'ry -

THAT'S WHAT FRIENDS ARE FOR

Music by BURT BACHARACH
Words by CAROLE BAYER SAGER

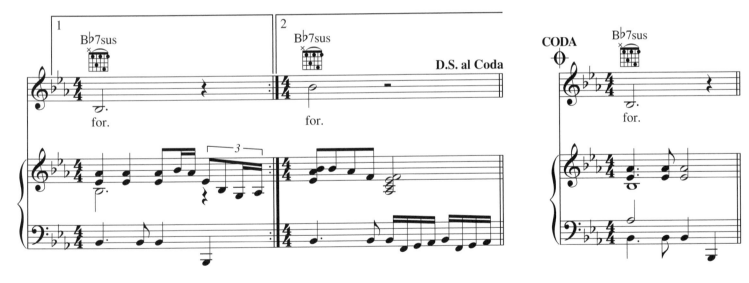

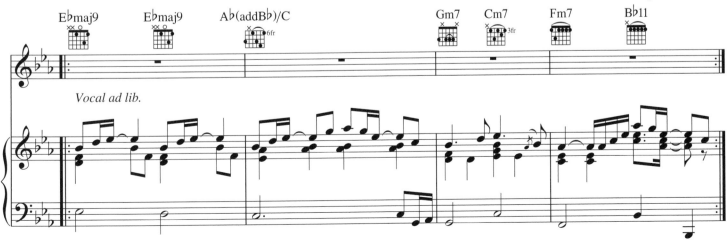

YOU ARE SO BEAUTIFUL

Words and Music by BILLY PRESTON
and BRUCE FISHER

Moderately slow, expressively

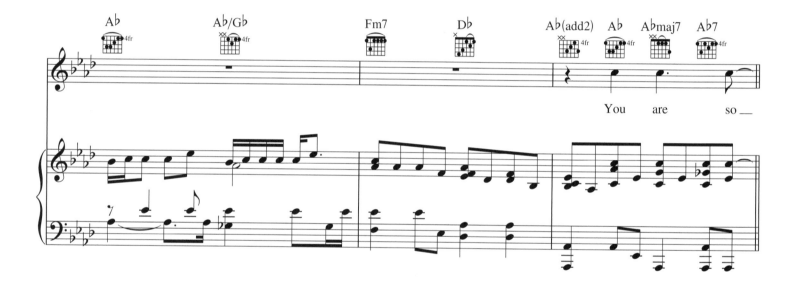

You are so __

__ beau - ti - ful __   to

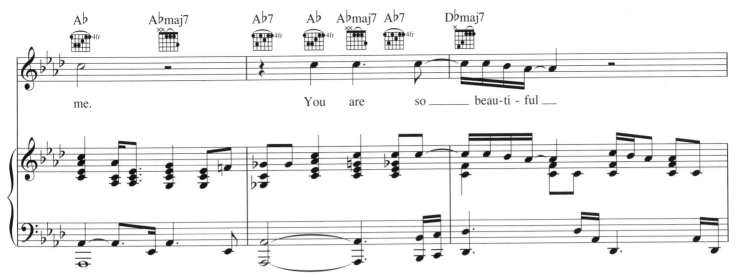

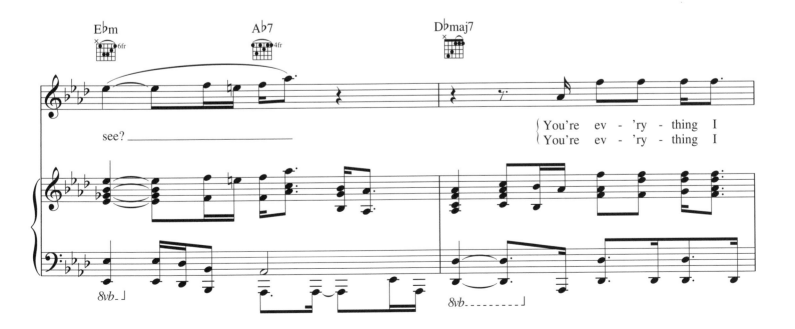

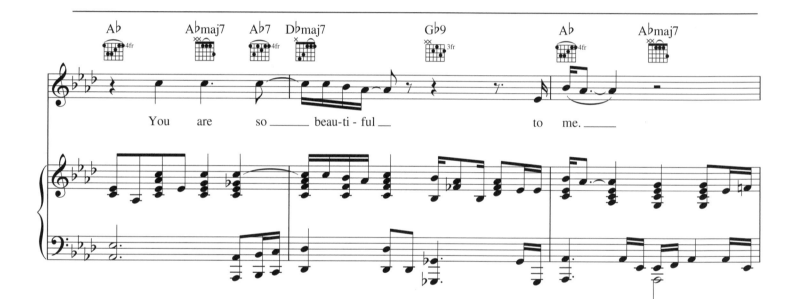

You are so _____ beau - ti - ful _____ to _____

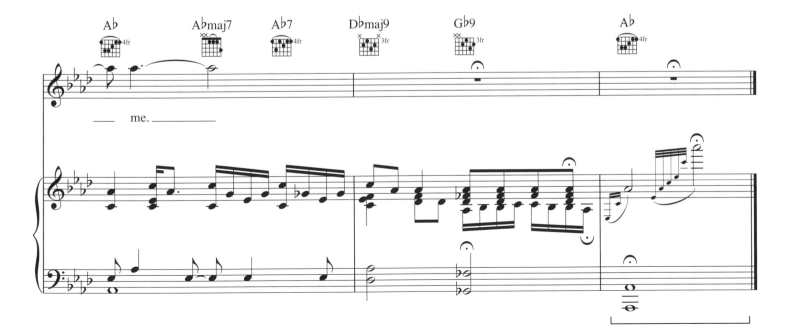

_____ me. _____

YOU'RE IN MY HEART

Words and Music by
ROD STEWART

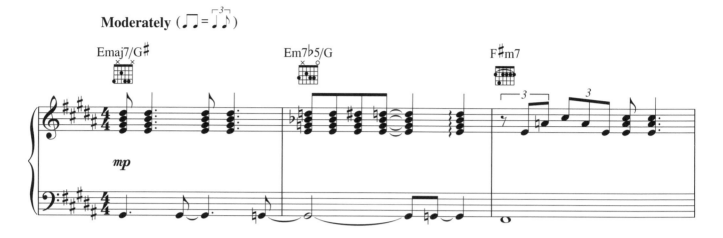

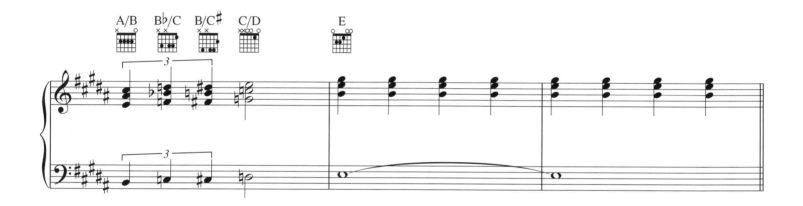

I did-n't know ___ what day it was ___ when you walked ___
I took all ___ those hab-its of yours that in the be-

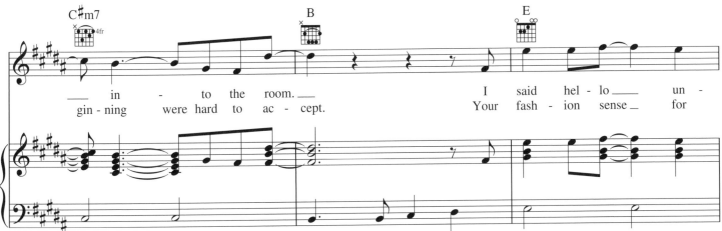

into the room. I said hel-lo un-
gin-ning were hard to ac-cept. Your fash-ion sense for

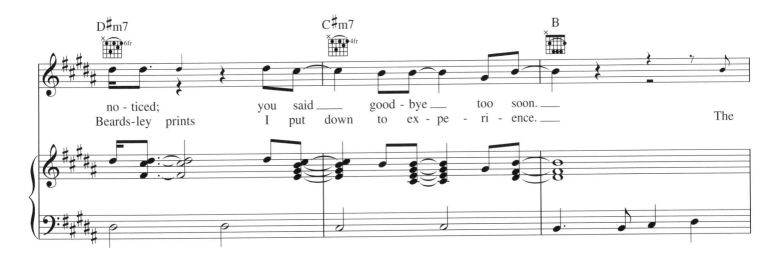

no-ticed; you said good-bye too soon.
Beards-ley prints I put down to ex-pe-ri-ence. The

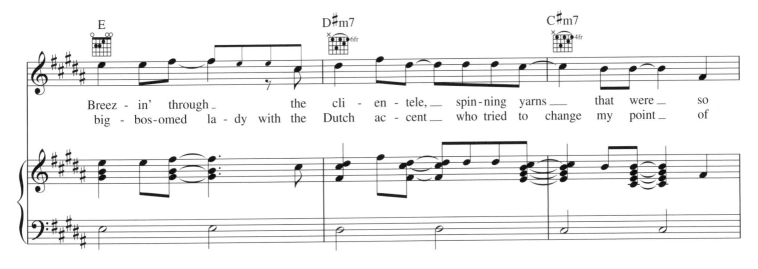

Breez-in' through the cli-en-tele, spin-ning yarns that were so
big-bos-omed la-dy with the Dutch ac-cent who tried to change my point of

lyr-i-cal, I real-ly must con-fess right here the at-
view, her ad lib lines were well re-hearsed, but my

My love for you __ is im-meas - ur - a - ble; my re-
You're an es - say in glam - our. Please par-don the gram - mar, but you're

spect for you __ im - mense. __ You're age - less, time - less,
ev - 'ry school - boy's dream. __ You're Cel - tic u - nit - ed,

lace and fine - ness; you're beau - ty and __ el - e - gance. __ You're a
but, ba - by, I've de - cid - ed you're the best team I've ev - er seen. And

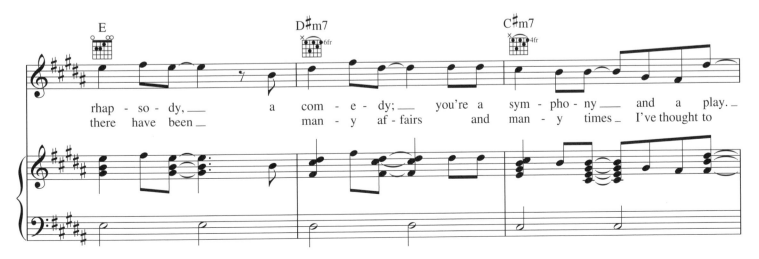

rhap - so - dy, __ a com - e - dy; __ you're a sym - pho - ny __ and a play.
there have been __ man - y af - fairs and man - y times __ I've thought to

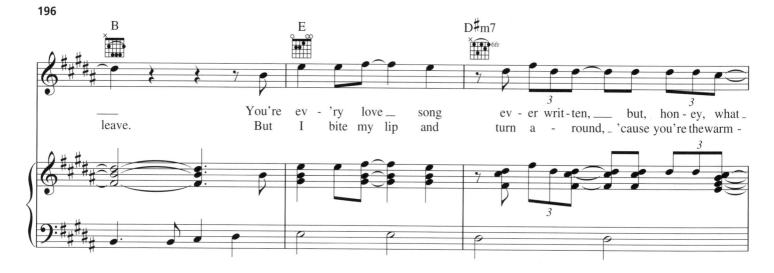

You're ev-'ry love __ song ev - er writ-ten, __ but, hon - ey, what __
leave. But I bite my lip and turn a - round, __ 'cause you're the warm -

__ do you see in me? __ You're in my heart; __
- est thing I've ev - er found. __ You're in my heart; __

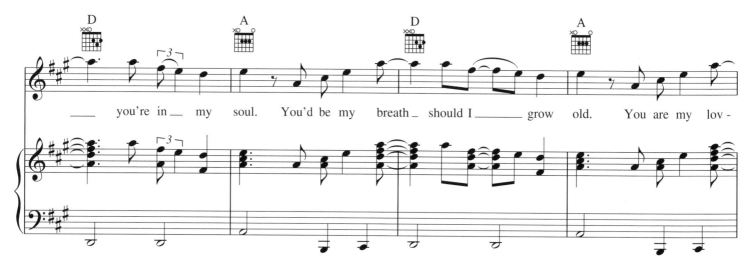

__ you're in __ my soul. You'd be my breath __ should I _____ grow old. You are my lov -

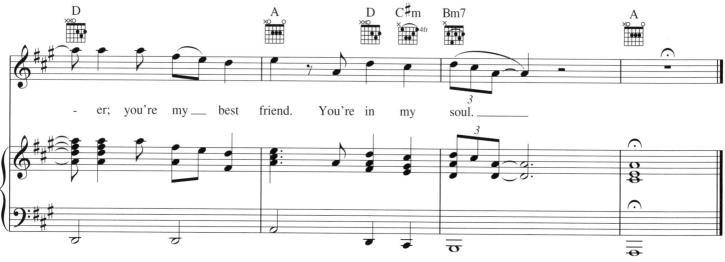

- er; you're my __ best friend. You're in my soul. _____

YOU'RE THE INSPIRATION

Words and Music by PETER CETERA
and DAVID FOSTER

Rock Ballad

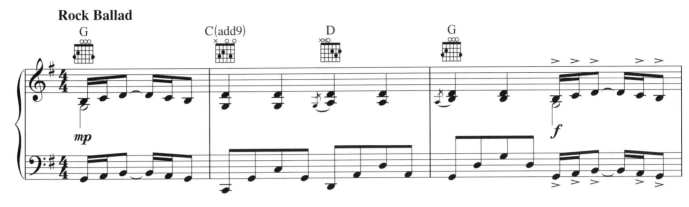

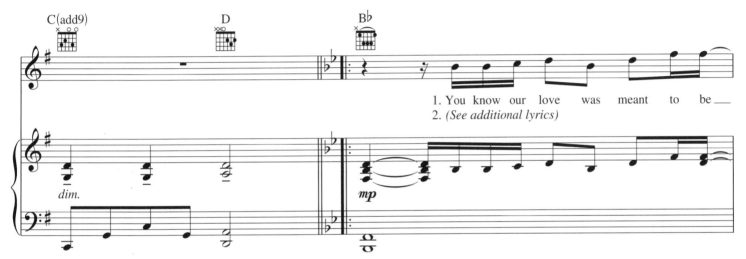

1. You know our love was meant to be ___
2. *(See additional lyrics)*

the kind of love ___ that lasts ___ for-

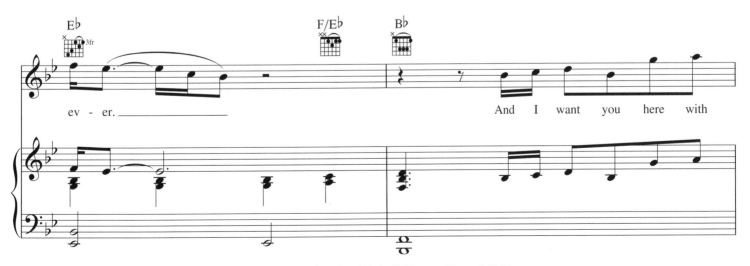

ev - er. ___ And I want you here with

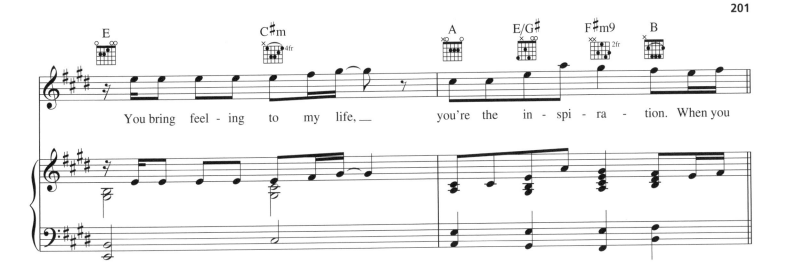

You bring feel - ing to my life, ___ you're the in - spi - ra - tion. When you

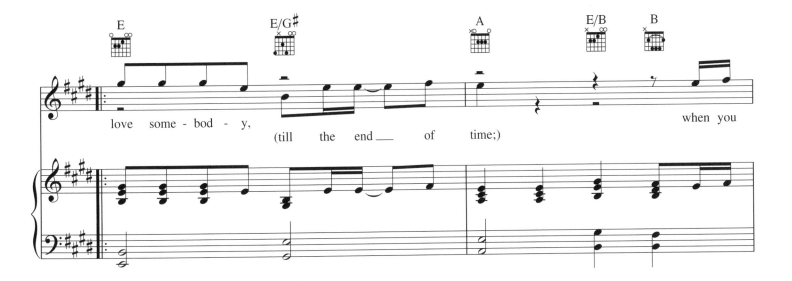

love some - bod - y, (till the end ___ of time;) when you

love some - bod - y, (al - ways on ___ my no one needs ___ you more than I. When you mind.)

Repeat ad lib. and Fade

Additional Lyrics

2. And I know (yes, I know)
   That it's plain to see
   We're so in love when we're together.
   Now I know (now I know)
   That I need you here with me
   From tonight until the end of time.
   You should know everywhere I go;
   Always on my mind, you're in my heart, in my soul.
   Chorus

YOU'VE GOT A FRIEND

Words and Music by
CAROLE KING

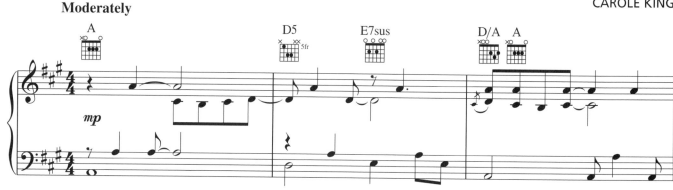

When you're down _____ and trou - bled and you
_____ a - bove _____ you should turn

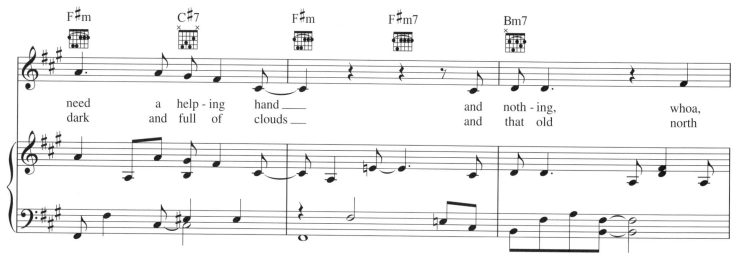

need a help - ing hand _____ and noth - ing, whoa,
dark and full of clouds _____ and that old north

noth - ing is go - ing right, _____
wind should be - gin _____ to blow, _____

close your eyes ___ and think of me ___ and soon I will ___ be ___ there ___
keep your head ___ to - geth - er ___ and call my name ___ out

___ loud, ___ now; ___ to bright - en up ___ e - ven your dark - est night. ___
soon I'll be knock - ing up - on ___ your door. ___

You just call ___ out my name, ___

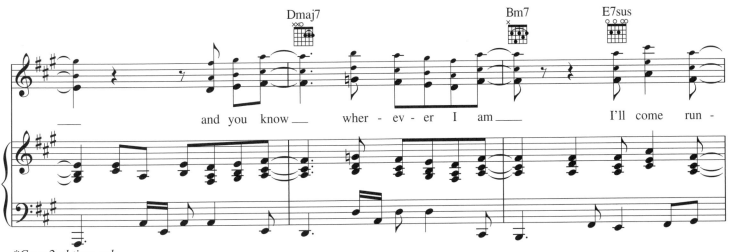

and you know ___ wher - ev - er I am ___ I'll come run -

*Cues 2nd time only

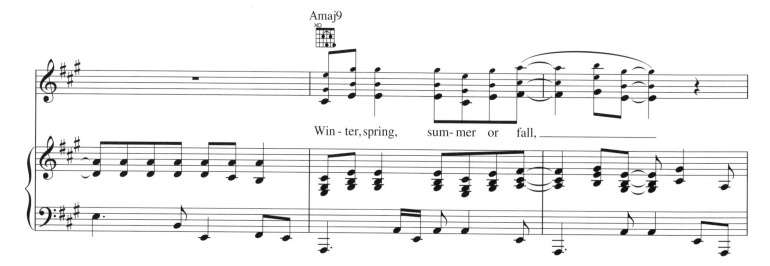

YOUR SONG

Words and Music by ELTON JOHN
and BERNIE TAUPIN

don't ___ have much mon - ey, _____ but ___
But the sun's been quite kind _____ while ___

boy, if ___ I did, _____ I'd buy ___ a big
I wrote ___ this song. ___ It's for peo - ple like

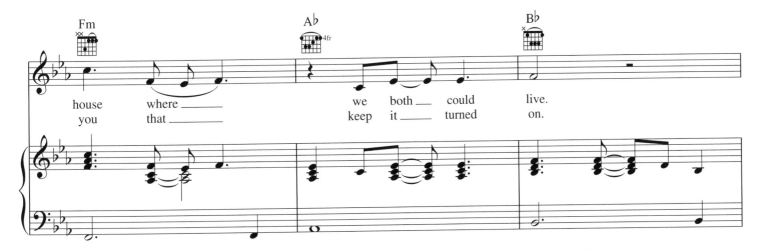

house where ___ we both ___ could live.
you that ___ keep it ___ turned on.

If I was a sculp - tor,
So ex - cuse me for - get - ting,

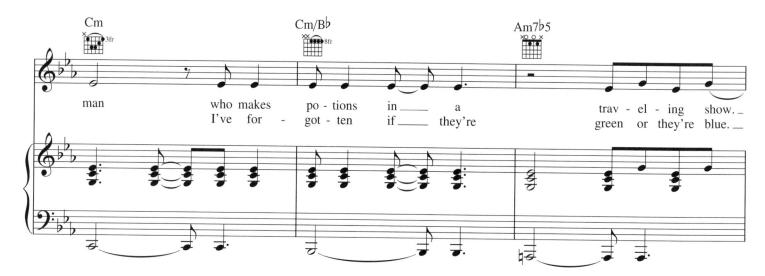

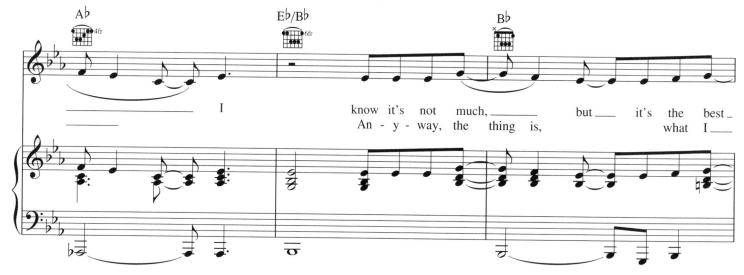

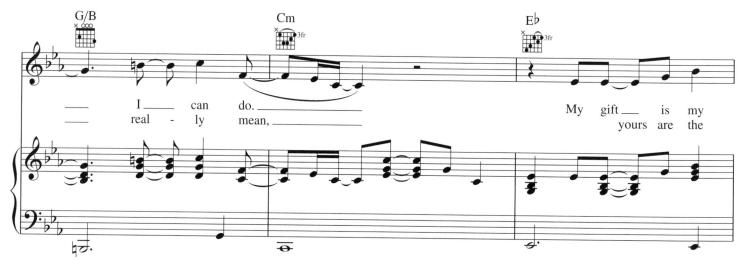

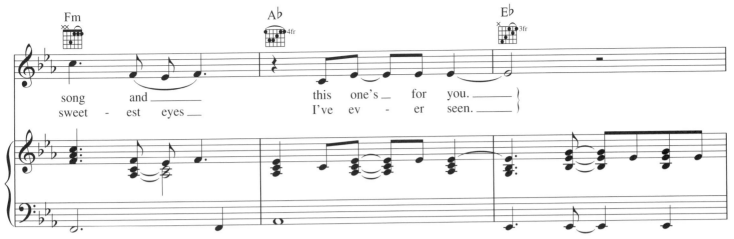

song and _____ this one's _ for you. _____
sweet - est eyes _____ I've ev - er seen. _____

And you _ can tell ev - 'ry - bod - y

this _ is your song. _____ It may _ be quite _

_____ sim - ple, but _____ now that it's done, _____

I hope you don't mind, _____ I hope you don't mind _____ that I put _____ down in

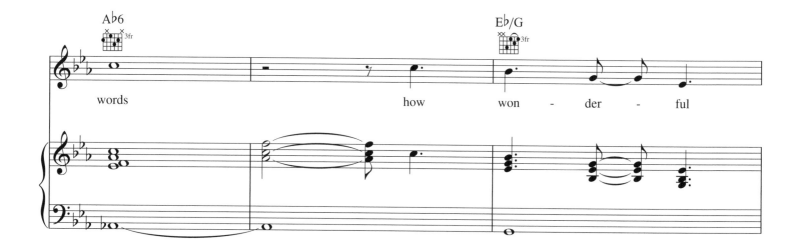

words _____ how won - der - ful

life is _____ while you're _____ in _____ the world. _____

(D.C.)

I hope you don't mind, I hope you don't mind ___ that I put ___ down in

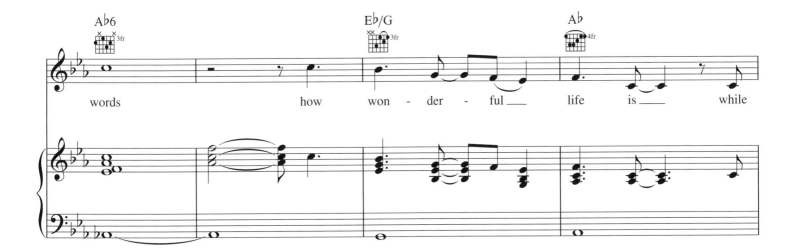

words how won - der - ful ___ life is ___ while

you're ___ in ___ the world. ___

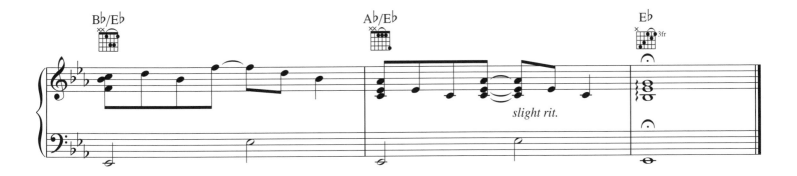

slight rit.

THE BEST EVER

COLLECTION
ARRANGED FOR PIANO, VOICE AND GUITAR

150 of the Most Beautiful Songs Ever
150 ballads
00360735 ....$27.00

150 More of the Most Beautiful Songs Ever
150 songs
00311318 ....$29.99

More of the Best Acoustic Rock Songs Ever
69 tunes
00311738 ....$19.95

Best Acoustic Rock Songs Ever
65 acoustic hits
00310984 ....$19.95

Best Big Band Songs Ever
68 big band hits
00359129 ....$17.99

Best Blues Songs Ever
73 blues tunes
00312874 ....$19.99

Best Broadway Songs Ever
83 songs
00309155 ....$24.99

More of the Best Broadway Songs Ever
82 songs
00311501 ....$22.95

Best Children's Songs Ever
96 songs
00310358 ....$19.99

Best Christmas Songs Ever
69 holiday favorites
00359130 ....$24.99

Best Classic Rock Songs Ever
64 hits
00310800 ....$22.99

Best Classical Music Ever
86 classical favorites
00310674 (Piano Solo) $19.95

The Best Country Rock Songs Ever
52 hits
00118881 ....$19.99

Best Country Songs Ever
78 classic country hits
00359135 ....$19.99

Best Disco Songs Ever
50 songs
00312565 ....$19.99

Best Dixieland Songs Ever
90 songs
00312326 ....$19.99

Best Early Rock 'n' Roll Songs Ever
74 songs
00310816 ....$19.95

Best Easy Listening Songs Ever
75 mellow favorites
00359193 ....$19.95

Best Gospel Songs Ever
80 gospel songs
00310503 ....$19.99

Best Hymns Ever
118 hymns
00310774 ....$18.99

Best Jazz Standards Ever
77 jazz hits
00311641 ....$19.95

More of the Best Jazz Standards Ever
74 beloved jazz hits
00311023 ....$19.95

Best Latin Songs Ever
67 songs
00310355 ....$19.99

Best Love Songs Ever
65 favorite love songs
00359198 ....$19.95

Best Movie Songs Ever
71 songs
00310063 ....$19.99

Best Praise & Worship Songs Ever
80 all-time favorites
00311057 ....$22.99

More of the Best Praise & Worship Songs Ever
76 songs
00311800 ....$24.99

Best R&B Songs Ever
66 songs
00310184 ....$19.95

Best Rock Songs Ever
63 songs
00490424 ....$18.95

Best Songs Ever
72 must-own classics
00359224 ....$24.99

Best Soul Songs Ever
70 hits
00311427 ....$19.95

Best Standards Ever, Vol. 1 (A-L)
72 beautiful ballads
00359231 ....$17.95

Best Standards Ever, Vol. 2 (M-Z)
73 songs
00359232 ....$17.99

More of the Best Standards Ever, Vol. 1 (A-L)
76 all-time favorites
00310813 ....$17.95

More of the Best Standards Ever, Vol. 2 (M-Z)
75 stunning standards
00310814 ....$17.95

Best Torch Songs Ever
70 sad and sultry favorites
00311027 ....$19.95

Best Wedding Songs Ever
70 songs
00311096 ....$19.95

Prices, contents and availability subject to change without notice. Not all products available outside the U.S.A.

7777 W. BLUEMOUND RD. P.O. BOX 13819 MILWAUKEE, WI 53213

Visit us online for complete songlists at
www.halleonard.com